Collins

REMARKABLE BIRDS | *Stephen Moss*

**For Neil McKillop and Daniel Osorio, my
long-standing birding companions.
May they eventually see every bird in this book.**

HarperCollins Publishers Ltd.
77-85 Fulham Palace Road
London
W6 8JB

The Collins website address is: www.collins.co.uk
Collins is a registered trademark of HarperCollins Publishers Ltd.

First published in 2007

A catalogue record for this book is available from the British Library.

ISBN 978 0 00 723025 9

Collins uses papers that are natural, renewable and recyclable
products made from wood grown in sustainable forests. The
manufacturing processes conform to the environmental regulations
of the country of origin.

Cover design by Emma Jern
Design by 'OMEDESIGN
Edited by Hugh Brazier
Proofread by Simon Pooley
Index by Lisa Footit
Colour reproduction by Colourscan, Singapore
Printed and bound in Malaysia by Imago

CONTENTS

Remarkable, adj. (Collins)
1. Worthy of note or attention
2. Unusual, striking, or extraordinary

Either of the definitions and any of these adjectives could apply to the 100 species of bird featured in this book. Each has been chosen for a particular quality – or set of qualities – that makes it stand out amongst the world's other 9,900 or so kinds of bird (each of which is, in its own way, special).

So what is it that makes these particular 100 birds stand out from the rest? One reason is that they have been chosen by an informal panel of expert birders, ornithologists and conservationists from all over the world. Representatives from almost 40 countries and territories – covering all six of the world's permanently inhabited continents – were asked to list the ten species they considered remarkable.

Though they were encouraged to include birds they considered 'unmissable', 'iconic', 'unique' or 'highly sought-after', they were free to decide their own criteria for inclusion. They were also asked to include personal favourites – after all, given that being 'remarkable' is a highly subjective quality, we wanted to encourage people to nominate their own favourites.

The results came in, together with some wonderfully evocative justifications for these particular choices (see the selection of quotes). Well over 500 different species were nominated in all, but certain ones kept coming to the top of the pile.

Choosing the final list was not easy: we tried not to include more than two species from each group or family as, otherwise, there would be a surplus of cranes, eagles and macaws! This did mean, however, that some wonderful birds – from Siberian Crane to Steller's Sea Eagle, and Red Kite to European Robin – are sadly not included in the final selection.

In other cases, especially with large families with a range of remarkable species such as parrots and penguins, the panel's choice was necessarily somewhat arbitrary. Certainly birds that are the only representative of their family – such as the Hoatzin, Kagu, Sunbittern and Oilbird – tended to get more nominations than those with a wider selection of relatives.

As the writer, it was then up to me to convey – in a few hundred words – what makes these birds so remarkable. I hope you think I have succeeded. And if your own 'remarkable bird' is not included, please do check out the website www.collins.co.uk/remarkablebirds and give us your thoughts. I look forward to reading your suggestions!

Stephen Moss
Somerset, December 2006

INTRODUCTION

LAMMERGEIER

As a young boy on the slopes of Mount Meru in Tanzania, our big brothers used to scare us by saying that the bird was so powerful that it could easily lift away small notorious boys who did not behave properly. From those early days I respected the bird and it kept in my mind up to now at 60 years old.

Paul Nnyiti, Tanzania

RESPLENDENT QUETZAL

Because of the look on its face, its trusting and fragile nature, the breathtaking flight in sunlight, the way it hangs vertically to feed, the fact that its presence indicates that the cloud forests are still there, it brings peace and hope.

Charlotte Elton, Panama

CONGO PEAFOWL

Deep in the forested depths of equatorial Africa's Congo basin exists one of the world's most secretive and enigmatic birds – a dream bird of mine since I was a teenager. Last year I embarked on a personal odyssey to seek it out. Taking a two-hour private plane trip straight into the heart of the Congo, I walked 170 km over 18 days (often through waist-deep water) before finally stumbling across the bird, one of the greatest 20 seconds of my life. I know of no other living ornithologists who have seen it.

Callan Cohen, South Africa

BEWICK'S SWAN

I love to watch the wild swans concentrating in the fields around my house during migration. The sky is filled with flocks during spring and fall for several weeks. The white against the blue sky is beautiful. Their sounds fill the air.

Kerrie Wilcox, Canada

WALLCREEPER

Based on the buzz when I finally saw it: whilst visiting Neuschwanstein (an outrageous fairytale castle in Bavaria), I was standing on a bridge across a gorge when something below caught my attention. Putting my binoculars on it, I almost fell off the bridge when I saw its crimson wings flicking and realised what it was. My girlfriend says I didn't stop grinning for the rest of the day.

Ian Burfield, the Netherlands

WILSON'S BIRD-OF-PARADISE

The vibrancy of its colours, the uniqueness of its blue skull-cap and its astonishing tameness when at its display ground are unparalleled. Add to this its remote location deep in rainforest on an obscure Papuan island, and I was as spellbound as David Attenborough and Alfred Russell Wallace were before me.

Guy Dutson, Australia

SELECTION OF QUOTES

BOHEMIAN WAXWING

Unpredictable and unbelievably beautiful, Waxwings are a godsend on cold dull winter days. They're also one of the best ambassadors for birding, persuading even the most stolid non-naturalist to notice them. It would be difficult to improve on the colour scheme – a real designer's bird!

Brett Westwood, UK

NIGHTINGALE

I have a letter written by my great-grandfather explaining how much he enjoyed listening to it, and now it builds its nest in my own garden!

Josep del Hoyo, Spain

RED KNOT

One of the most fascinating birds of the world because of its extreme migrations, often occurring in flocks of tens or even hundreds of thousands of birds, and its most beautiful song performances high in the air over the snow-covered high-arctic tundra.

Hans Meltofte, Denmark

WANDERING ALBATROSS

A truly awe-inspiring species so aptly named. Able to 'wander' the storm-ravished southern oceans effortlessly. Leaves you gasping with disbelief when first encountered.

Tony Palliser, Australia

COMMON SWIFT

Often you realise what you really value only when it's no longer there. Every year I am reminded of this when I realise that I haven't seen a swift around my house for a couple of days and that it will be another nine months before these magnificent creatures return. What a bird!

Ade Long, UK

ARCTIC TERN

Mid-June on the island of Inner Farne off the coast of Northumberland. The air is full of sharp chattering calls and a blizzard of birds skim through my vision. At my feet, Arctic Terns are feeding newly hatched chicks in their nest scrapes. I can only stand and gaze in awe at these remarkable birds which see more daylight than any other animal on earth, and have recently just flown over ten thousand miles from the Antarctic to return here to breed. Not remarkable, astonishing.

Chris Watson, UK

SELECTION OF QUOTES

Many people have helped me compile this book, including friends and birding contacts who sent me their choices and comments at the start of the project: John Aitchison, Mark Barrow, Bo Beolens, Keith Betton, Marek Borkowski, John A. Burton, Dominic Couzens, Chris Ellis, Jim Flegg, Mark Golley, Philip Griffin, Chris Harbard, Josep del Hoyo, Tony Marr, Derek Moore, Bridget Nicholls, Daniel Osorio, Richard Porter, Nigel Redman, Rod Standing, Chris Watson, Brett Westwood, Martin and Barbara Woodcock, and Mac Wright.

Thanks to an appeal by Ade Long at BirdLife International, who forwarded our questionnaire to the BirdLife partners, we received results from almost 40 different territories: **Europe** – Austria, Belgium, the Channel Islands, Croatia, Denmark, Ireland, Latvia, Malta, the Netherlands, Poland, Spain, Sweden, Switzerland, the UK; **North and South America** – Argentina, Bolivia, Canada, Ecuador, the Falkland Islands, Panama, Paraguay, the USA; **Asia** – Azerbaijan, China, Hong Kong, Iran, Nepal, Singapore; **Africa** – Tanzania, the Seychelles, South Africa; **Australasia and the Pacific** – Australia, Fiji, French Polynesia, New Caledonia, New Zealand.

The respondents also included Claudia Ahrens, Jacobo Araúz, Hem Sagar Baral, Gerard Bertrand, Wim Van den Bossche, Andrés Bosso, Ariel Brunner, Ian Burfield, Denis Cachia, Jimmy Choi, Callan Cohen, Alison Duncan, Guy Dutson, Michael Dvorak, Charlotte Elton, Ian Fraser, Itzel Fong Gadea, Alistair Gammell, Paul Green, Gilberto de la Guardia, Keith Harrison, Niall Hatch, Henning Heldbjerg, A. Bennett Hennessy, Cora Maria Herrera, Titu Shitembula Imboma, Eva Karner-Ranner, Saartjie Kidson, Oliver Komar, Lim Kim Seng, Ida Lui Sze Nga, Alan McBride, Jamshod Mansoori, Ieva Mardega, Carmen M. Martino, Michael Mills, Rosabel Miró, Peter Morris, Werner Müller, Grant Munro, Dr Jasmina Muzinic, Paul Nnyiti, Maria Olsson, Tony Palliser, Ber van Perlo, Philippe Raust, Laura Reyes, Julieta Rovi, Maurice Rumboll, Dr Alejandro Sanchez, Tatiana Santander, Nirmal Jivan Shah, Jérôme Spaggiari, Peter Sullivan, Joe Sultana, Elchin Sultanov, Lars Svensson, Michael Szabo, Tan Siew Kwang, Miliana Vukunisiga, Dan Wade, Gabor Wichmann, Kerrie Wilcox, Alberto Yanosky and H. Glyn Young. I'd also like to thank all at HarperCollins for helping to produce this book to their usual very high standards: Myles Archibald, Kirstie Addis, Julia Koppitz, Emily Pitcher, Fiona Marsh and Emma Jern.

And with special thanks to the wonderful Helen Brocklehurst who, having commissioned this book and worked on it with her customary enthusiasm and expertise, has moved on to the delights of 'popular non-fiction' – where she will undoubtedly be, as always, quietly successful.

ACKNOWLEDGEMENTS

The world's largest living bird is something of an anomaly in the avian world: a primitive, flightless giant with a kick like a mule, the largest eyes of any land-dwelling creature (it is beaten only by the giant squid of the ocean depths), and eyelashes that would put a catwalk model to shame.

The statistics of this super-heavyweight are true record-breakers: it is the world's tallest bird, reaching a height of up to 2.5 m; and the heaviest, weighing as much as 136 kg. The Ostrich dwarfs all but its closest relatives: the South American rheas, and the cassowaries and Emu of Australasia.

The Ostrich also lays the largest egg of any living bird – at 1.5 kg it is the rough equivalent of two-dozen chickens' eggs, and takes 45 minutes to boil. Yet because of the huge size of the bird itself, the egg represents less than 1.5 per cent of the adult's body-weight – making it relatively smaller than the egg of any other bird.

Today the Ostrich is confined to Africa south of the Sahara, but until the middle of the 20th century a tiny relict population hung on in the deserts of Arabia. Unfortunately the toll taken by hunting meant that, when conservation efforts were made to save this unique subspecies, it was too late. Attempts are now being made to reintroduce the Ostrich to parts of the Middle East, though, with that region's history of conflict, the chances of it surviving there may not be great.

The Ostrich is a textbook example of the benefits of flightlessness. By staying earthbound, the species has been able to massively increase both its size and its weight – in the case of the latter to about ten times that of the largest flying birds. Its huge, muscular legs enable it to foil any attack with a well-placed kick and, if all else fails, to run away at speeds of up to 70 km per hour. Another weapon against predators is its extraordinary eyesight.

With such an armoury of ways of avoiding attack, burying its head in the sand would appear to go against common sense; and indeed this is a myth, probably arising from its habit of sitting motionless with its head and neck stretched forward in the face of danger.

The Ostrich's reproductive habits are extraordinary too. Up to 78 eggs have been found in a single scrape in the ground (what an omelette that would make!), though this was the result of several females sharing one nest.

Not surprisingly, Ostriches have long been exploited for their flesh, eggs and magnificent feathers – the eggs being used for ornaments as well as for food. Ostrich meat is high in protein but low in fat, which in the late 20th century led to the spread of ostrich meat as a healthy alternative to beef. However, consumer reluctance and some financial scandals have led to an uncertain future for the industry in Europe.

The world's largest living bird – a true record-breaker

Struthio camelus | # OSTRICH

A FLEEING OSTRICH CAN COVER 100 METRES IN JUST FIVE SECONDS, ABOUT HALF THE TIME OF AN OLYMPIC SPRINTER, MAKING IT THE FASTEST CREATURE ON TWO LEGS

Imagine that a new organism has been discovered in the dense forests of a remote land in the southern hemisphere. Covered with a fine brown layer of what looks and feels like fur, it feeds by foraging around the dense undergrowth, eating insects and some vegetable matter. Almost exclusively nocturnal, it has very poor eyesight but extremely acute senses of hearing and especially smell.

Given this description, most scientists would guess that the species was a small mammal, perhaps related to the rodents or insectivores such as the hedgehogs. But that dense 'fur' is in fact modified feathers; the method used to find food involves a long, sensitive bill; and the creature lays enormous eggs. It is, therefore, undoubtedly a bird – though admittedly a very peculiar one: the Brown Kiwi.

The Brown Kiwi is one of three kiwi species endemic to the remote archipelago of New Zealand. Indeed, they are not merely endemic, but more closely associated with that country than any other living creature. Not only at home, but the world over, New Zealanders are known as 'kiwis'.

Despite their small size, ranging from 35 to 65 cm in length and weighing 1–4 kg, the kiwis' closest relatives are in fact the Ostrich, rheas, cassowaries and the Emu. Collectively known as ratites, these primitive birds share many characteristics, including several adaptations to a purely terrestrial existence.

So why are the kiwis so different from the rest of their family? The answer lies in the date that kiwis (and their now-extinct relatives, the moas) split from their closest relatives. This was as long as 70 million years ago, at the time that the vast super-continent of Gondwanaland was breaking up into the continents and islands we know today.

The most obvious clues to the kiwis' evolutionary origins are the huge size of their eggs and their long incubation periods. The egg of the Little Spotted Kiwi represents about one-quarter of the female's entire body-weight; and the incubation of the Brown Kiwi (carried out entirely by the male) lasts between two and three months. We can infer from these statistics that the kiwis' ancestors were considerably larger than today's birds, and that evolutionary pressure led to greatly reduced body size without having such a dramatic effect on the size of the egg.

Sadly, as with so many flightless birds confined to islands, all three species of kiwi (Little Spotted, Great Spotted and Brown) suffered greatly from becoming prey to introduced mammals and human settlers. The Maoris prided themselves on their ceremonial cloaks made from kiwi 'fur', while later settlers exploited them for meat and used the skins for muffs. Today only the Brown Kiwi survives in anything like its former range, and is the only member of its family still to be found on the North Island of New Zealand.

A Brown Kiwi in the dense undergrowth where it lives

Apteryx australis | # BROWN KIWI

KIWIS PUT ON HUGE AMOUNTS OF FAT BEFORE THE BREEDING SEASON. THIS ENABLES THE FEMALES TO CREATE SUCH ENORMOUS EGGS, AND THE MALES TO SURVIVE THE LONG PERIOD OF INCUBATION.

Emperor Penguins are popular not only with birders and ornithologists – everyone loves them.

Named for its regal stance (outranking its smaller relative the King Penguin), the world's largest penguin is a contender for the world's hardiest bird. It earns this honour by being the only creature that breeds during the harsh Antarctic winter, when temperatures regularly stay at least 40°C below freezing for six months or more. It is also one of only a handful of bird species whose breeding range is restricted to the Antarctic continent.

Emperors gather at their breeding colonies in early winter, just after the sea ice has begun to form. After an intricate courtship display followed by mating, a single egg is laid, which the female transfers to the male for incubation – his responsibility alone. He safeguards the egg by balancing it on top of his feet, where it can be protected by a fold of his skin.

For the next two months his sole task is to keep the egg warm; one slip and it will touch the frozen ice beneath his feet, and the whole breeding attempt will need to be postponed for another year. During this incubation period (the longest continuous spell by any bird) he does not eat, and only moves by shuffling around the flock to find a slightly warmer – or at least less cold – spot amongst his fellow penguins.

Finally, after about 67 days, the egg hatches and the baby emerges to face the hazards of the

The march of the Emperor Penguins

world. Only when the female returns from feeding does the male finally pass over the tiny chick, and then sets off on the long trek back to the ocean to feed – a journey of more than 140 km.

So why has the Emperor Penguin developed such a bizarre breeding cycle? The reason is the time it takes for such a large bird to raise a chick: if they left it until spring to lay their eggs, the young would not have grown large enough to survive through the following winter. Only by braving the freezing 'eternal night' of the Antarctic winter can the Emperors give their offspring a chance of survival.

Emperor Penguins are record-breakers in other ways, too. They can dive deeper than any other bird, and have been reliably recorded at depths of more than 250 m (with some claims of up to 500 m). They hold the record for staying underwater: at least 18 and perhaps as many as 22 minutes on a single breath, though a more typical dive lasts between three and six minutes. They weigh between 25 and 40 kg, and can grow to a height of 115 cm – about the same as a typical ten-year-old child.

The world population of Emperor Penguins has been estimated at between 135,000 and 175,000 pairs, and currently the species is not considered to be globally threatened. However, the rapid onset of climate change, with its effects apparently greater at the two poles, could have serious consequences for this species.

EMPEROR PENGUIN | *Aptenodytes forsteri*

IN 2005 A FRENCH-MADE DOCUMENTARY FILM, *MARCH OF THE PENGUINS*, BECAME THE SUMMER HIT AT THE US BOX OFFICE, AND WAS CHAMPIONED BY THE RIGHT-WING CHRISTIAN LOBBY AS A CELEBRATION OF FIDELITY AND MONOGAMY!

In the 1981 film *On Golden Pond*, in which Katharine Hepburn won a record-breaking fourth Oscar, and Henry Fonda finally won his first, the Common Loon also plays a powerful role. The drama of family relationship and reconciliation is played out to a chorus of loons, whose melancholy and haunting calls add to the febrile atmosphere.

On the other side of the Atlantic, more than 30 years earlier, children's writer Arthur Ransome also used the species – though with its British rather than American name – as the backdrop to his dramatic tale *Great Northern?*, in which a band of holidaying children foil a dastardly egg-collector.

Two such different fictional uses of the bird are proof of this species' charismatic character, which is due not least to its striking monochrome plumage and extraordinary call. The second-largest of the five species in its family, it shares with them an ancient lineage that has been traced back 65 million years to the Age of Dinosaurs, and which has traditionally put them at or near the front of field guides.

Today, it has a markedly Nearctic (North American) distribution, breeding widely across Canada, the northern USA, Greenland and Iceland, with only a handful of breeding records elsewhere in Europe, including Britain. The species winters mainly at sea, on the Pacific and Atlantic coasts of North America and off northwest Europe.

Divers are the most aquatic and charismatic of birds

Divers are, along with the grebes, the most aquatic of all birds, spending virtually the whole time (apart from when nesting) on the water. The feet are well back on the body to gain maximum propulsion when diving. As a result they are ungainly on land, where they hobble about or use both legs to propel themselves forwards like a particularly clumsy frog. On the water, they sit very low, with the waves sometimes lapping across their backs.

As their British name suggests, they dive often and for long periods, to depths of up to 10 m, in search of a wide range of fish from minnows to cod, and some plants, amphibians and invertebrates.

The name 'loon' has entered our language as an insult, but its derivation is uncertain. Some sources claim that it comes from a Scandinavian word meaning 'lame' or 'clumsy'; others propose a Scottish origin, relating to its call.

The wide repertoire of calls has been described as everything from 'uncontrolled, idiotic laughter' to 'melancholy and haunting', depending perhaps on the mood of the listener. The sound has long been associated with the coming of rain, particularly by the Thompson Indians of British Columbia. In Scotland, divers' calls are sometimes regarded as an evil omen.

The reality is more prosaic: loons are monogamous and pair for life; the calls are part of a ritual of courtship display to maintain the pair bond.

GREAT NORTHERN DIVER | *Gavia immer*

UNTIL THE 18TH CENTURY THE WORD 'DIVER' WAS USED FOR A WIDE RANGE OF WATERBIRDS; ONLY THEN DID IT BECOME ADOPTED FOR THE MEMBERS OF THE *GAVIIDAE* FAMILY

At 3.6 m, the wingspan of the Wandering Albatross is the longest of any bird in the world. Along with its closest relatives, the species also has the longest incubation period of any bird, between 75 and 85 days – though not, as with the Emperor Penguin, in one continuous stretch by a single parent.

It also has the longest fledging period of any flying bird: 280 days, which explains why this and the other larger albatrosses raise a single chick only every two years. For this reason the pair bond is very strong. Wandering Albatrosses usually breed for the first time at about eleven years old, and the pair bond lasts for life – 50 years or more.

The Wandering Albatross's ability to stay on the wing for weeks on end, as it cruises the vast, open oceans of the southern hemisphere, has led to a wealth of superstition and folklore. The best-known mention of it is Samuel Taylor Coleridge's poem *The Rime of the Ancient Mariner*, in which the eponymous sailor kills an albatross following his ship.

As a result, the mariner, his ship and all his fellow sailors fall under a curse, and he is forced to wear the dead bird around his neck. The wind drops, the ship is becalmed and all aboard suffer terrible thirst, summed up in the poem's most famous quatrain:

Water, water, every where,
And all the boards did shrink;
Water, water, every where,
Nor any drop to drink.

The poem has so much entered popular culture that we still refer to a person's unwanted burden as an 'albatross'.

Like many seabirds, albatrosses are exceptionally long-lived, and under normal circumstances have very low annual mortality rates. However, the arrival of the global fishing industry in the remote waters of the Southern Ocean has changed everything, and may threaten the very existence of this magnificent bird.

The problem is the main method used to catch fish, which involves stretching out lines of nets baited with hooks for several kilometres behind each trawler (known as long-lining). Although highly effective as a fishing method, long-lining is lethal to birds that feed from the surface of the sea such as albatrosses. Seeing a fish, they plunge down and grab it, only to find themselves impaled on a sharp hook. Death is slow, painful and almost inevitable.

The Wandering Albatross – a bird
steeped in superstition and folklore

WANDERING ALBATROSS | *Diomedea exulans*

DESPITE A WORLDWIDE CAMPAIGN AGAINST LONG-LINING, SUPPORTED BY CELEBRITIES SUCH AS JERRY HALL AND QUEEN NOOR OF JORDAN, THE SITUATION CONTINUES TO WORSEN

In the stark, bright, white environment of the Antarctic, what could be more appropriate than a bird that – apart from its dark eyes, bill and legs – has a completely snow-white plumage? Huge numbers of aptly named Snow Petrels often appear behind a ship like some heavenly vision, resembling snowflakes falling from the sky.

Confined to Antarctica and the surrounding oceans (the northernmost colony is on South Georgia), Snow Petrels usually occur in areas with between 10 and 50 per cent ice cover. These provide plenty of opportunities for them to land on ice floes or larger icebergs, for, unlike other petrels, this species rarely, if ever, alights on water. Instead it feeds by picking off morsels from the surface of the ocean, sometimes plunging down momentarily into the sea to catch its prey.

Its diet consists mainly of the staple food of so many Antarctic creatures, krill, along with other small fish. However, Snow Petrels do sometimes scavenge whale or seal carcasses – where they are often joined by another all-white Antarctic species, albeit a less attractive one, the Snowy Sheathbill.

During the brief austral summer, Snow Petrels gather in vast concentrations at their breeding colonies, where they nest in rocky crevices

The Snow Petrel is, as its name suggests, one of the whitest of all birds

on cliff faces. One such, deep in the heart of the Antarctic continent, is shared with thousands of Antarctic Petrels. Both species are at the mercy of predatory South Polar Skuas, which take both eggs and chicks, severely reducing the chances of breeding success.

Another thing that makes the petrels' life even tougher is the very harsh climate, made worse by the altitude of some of its colonies – in one case more than 2,400 m above sea level. Ironically, the current amelioration of the polar climate poses an even greater threat to the species: warmer waters may bring about a major decline in krill stocks, thus making it harder for the petrels to survive at all.

Recent studies have suggested that the two races of Snow Petrel may in fact be separate species, as they appear not to interbreed where their ranges overlap. The only way to tell them apart is that the aptly-named *confusa* race is slightly larger.

During the courtship, the female puts the male through a series of tests, flying around the rocky cliffs in an aerial dance, twisting and turning as she dares her mate to pursue. Either he keeps up and stays the course, in which case she will let him mate with her, or he gives up and looks for a less demanding female.

SNOW PETREL | *Pagodroma nivea*

ONE OF THE MOST BEAUTIFUL NATURAL SIGHTS OF ANTARCTICA IS ONE THAT IS RARELY WITNESSED: THE COURTSHIP DISPLAY OF A PAIR OF SNOW PETRELS

In Greek myth, Phaethon, whose father was the sun-god Helios, was permitted to drive the chariot of the sun for a single day. However, he drove so fast that the earth was almost set on fire, and as a punishment the great god Zeus struck him down with a thunderbolt. His fate is commemorated in the generic name of all three species of tropicbird, whose flight is arguably the most graceful of all birds.

If a tern can be said to be 'a gull that has died and gone to heaven', then what superlatives remain for this stunning creature? The combination of long wings, longer tail and striking black-and-white plumage, contrasting with a bright blood-red bill creates a bird whose buoyant beauty takes the breath away.

Sailors have given tropicbirds less flattering names: 'Marlinspike', referring to the similarity between the long central tail-feathers and a nautical tool, and 'Bosunbird', which apparently originates from the similarity between the bird's call and the sound of a bosun's pipe.

Like their close relatives the frigatebirds, all three tropicbird species have the capacity to remain airborne for days on end, taking advantage of their low body-weight and powerful wings. Their relationship with frigatebirds extends into a constant battle of wits: the piratical frigatebirds frequently chase the smaller and more elegant tropicbirds in order to make them regurgitate or drop their food.

As with so many seabirds, tropicbirds spend the vast majority of their lives out on the open ocean, only returning to land to breed in loose colonies. Like many tropical species they breed when they can, so in ideal conditions they may do so more than once in a single calendar year. During breeding, when they must return to land, their elegance vanishes: with tiny legs they can only move around by waddling about in an unflattering manner.

Once tropicbirds leave the nest, they disperse far and wide, with records of Red-billed Tropicbirds (whose breeding colonies are mainly in the Caribbean, Galápagos and South Atlantic Ocean) as far away as the British Isles, Pakistan and Israel.

Tropicbirds have few natural enemies, though, like other oceanic island birds, they have been badly affected by cats and rats introduced to their breeding locations. Human persecution has also been a problem – mainly for their long feathers, which are used for ornamental purposes. The only breeding population on the eastern side of the Atlantic, on the Cape Verde Islands, has been hard hit by fishermen, declining from about a thousand pairs in the late 1960s to just over a hundred pairs today.

The buoyant beauty of the Red-billed Tropicbird as it approaches its nest in the Galápagos

Phaethon aethereus | # RED-BILLED TROPICBIRD

TROPICBIRDS USUALLY FEED FAR OUT TO SEA, WITH THE BIRDS PLUNGING DOWN TO THE SURFACE TO GRAB SMALL SQUID AND FLYING FISH, SOMETIMES HOVERING OVER THE WATER BEFORE GOING FOR THE KILL

The largest of the world's seven species of pelican – with some males tipping the scales at 13 kg and boasting a wingspan of more than 3 m – the Dalmatian Pelican is a truly awe-inspiring sight, though unfortunately a fairly rare one. Although it breeds from the Danube Delta in eastern Europe all the way to China, its range, like that of so many species dependent on large areas of wetland, is highly fragmented and discontinuous.

When breeding, they regurgitate food – mainly carp, pike and perch – for their young, which have to reach inside the huge bill of their parent in order to feed – a bizarre sight. At this time of year the adult's gular pouch (the flap extending beneath its bill) is blood-red, which appears to have given rise to the legend that the parent pelican splits open her breast to feed her young on blood.

The Dalmatian Pelican has suffered a rapid decline during the past hundred years or so, with the main threats being the loss of its wetland habitat, direct persecution (often by fishermen who believe it threatens their livelihood) and disturbance – including that from tourists using speedboats to get close-up views.

Hunting is also a problem: pelican bills are used for a variety of purposes, including sheaths for hunting knives, tobacco pouches, and in Mongolia as an implement to wipe the sweat from horses.

As a result of this, by the early 1990s the world population had dropped to fewer than 3,000 pairs and the species was threatened with extinction. Fortunately, conservation measures appear to have reversed this decline, and although the species is still giving cause for concern it is now classified as 'Vulnerable'.

Like most members of their family, Dalmatian Pelicans are gregarious and sociable, often resting in groups on sandbanks when not searching for food. However, they rarely gather in large flocks like their close relative the Great White Pelican, and generally fish singly, or occasionally in twos or threes.

Dalmatian Pelicans have also formed a symbiotic relationship with another master fisherman, the Great Cormorant. On the Prespa Lakes in northern Greece cormorants have been observed diving under the water, closely followed by a pelican fluttering across the surface. Just as the pelican plunges down to catch a fish, so the cormorant surfaces with a fish of its own. It is thought that the cormorant benefits from the pelican's ability to find good feeding places, while the pelican benefits from the cormorant chasing the fish to the surface.

A pair of Dalmatian Pelicans fishing in Macedonia

Pelecanus crispus | # DALMATIAN PELICAN

DALMATIAN PELICANS REQUIRE LARGE AMOUNTS OF FISH — MORE THAN 1 KG PER DAY — WHICH THEY OBTAIN BY SURFACE-FEEDING. THIS IS USUALLY DONE IN FRESH WATER, BUT OCCASIONALLY THEY FISH OFFSHORE

Once a year, usually sometime in the month of August, a group of fishermen from the Hebridean island of Lewis (off the northwest coast of Scotland) go on an expedition. But fish are not their quarry – instead they are on the 'guga hunt', harvesting up to 2,000 young gannets from the remote island of Sula Sgeir.

The guga hunt is the only surviving legal cull of birds in the United Kingdom. It goes back hundreds – perhaps thousands – of years, to a time when the protein and fat from these birds would have meant the difference between life and death for some remote communities. The islanders of St Kilda not only paid their rent in gannet skins and feathers, they even used the birds as slippers, discarding the battered skins after a few weeks' use.

A metre in length, and weighing up to 3.6 kg, the Northern Gannet (so called to distinguish it from its two southern-hemisphere relatives, the Cape and Australasian Gannets) is the largest seabird regularly to breed in the north Atlantic.

Everything about the gannet appears designed for a single job: to hunt fish by plunge-diving. The wings are long and pointed, enabling them to be folded on impact with the water. The eyes, like those of birds of prey, face forward so that the bird can judge distances more accurately. And the feet are set well back on the body, making gannets somewhat clumsy on land but allowing them to propel themselves to depths of 25 m beneath the surface of the sea.

One peculiar result of the need to be as streamlined as possible is that gannets, unlike most other birds, have no brood patch on their belly (the bare area of skin which helps keep the eggs warm). Instead, gannets actually stand on their egg to transfer heat through the soles of their feet; for this reason, the shells of their eggs are remarkably thick.

As a result of nesting so close to one another, gannets have developed a complex series of breeding rituals. They use their sharp, fearsome bills not only to ward off rivals, but also as part of a pair-bonding display known as 'sky-pointing', in which male and female direct their bills straight up in the air while emitting a variety of strange noises.

Probably the best-known gannetry in the world is the island of Bass Rock, in the Firth of Forth within sight of the city of Edinburgh. Here thousands of gannets create an awesome spectacle of sight and sound. However, one visiting photographer noted the contrast between the almost surreal beauty of gannets hanging in the blue sky above Bass Rock, and the reality of their extraordinary smell – the toilet habits of the species leaving something to be desired.

Gannets overhead, as they prepare to plunge-dive

Morus bassanus | NORTHERN GANNET

NESTING IN VAST COLONIES (THE LARGEST, WITH OVER 60,000 PAIRS, IS ON ST KILDA), THE GANNET'S STRIKING PLUMAGE AND SPECTACULAR HABITS MAKE IT ONE OF THE WORLD'S TRULY ICONIC SPECIES

'The natural history of these islands is eminently curious, and well deserves attention.' So wrote Charles Darwin, in October 1845, in the pages of his journal on the voyage of *HMS Beagle*. He was, of course, referring to the Galápagos Archipelago, where he found some of the most bizarre and unusual creatures he had ever seen.

One such was the Flightless (also often known as Galápagos) Cormorant, found on just two islands in the west of that famous archipelago. Here, the upwellings from two cold-water currents – the Cromwell and the Humboldt – are greater than elsewhere in the Galápagos, providing an abundance of fish, octopus and squid on which the cormorants like to feed.

Like so many Galápagos birds, this cormorant has diverged markedly from its mainland relatives. After all, of the world's 10,000 or so species of birds, fewer than 50 species have lost the power of flight.

The Flightless Cormorant's inability to fly makes it amongst the most sedentary of all birds, rarely moving more than 1 km from where it breeds. Indeed, even though the islands on which it lives – Fernandina and Isabela – are only a few kilometres apart, birds hardly ever travel between the m.

As is often the case with birds of isolated oceanic islands, the Flightless Cormorant dispensed with its ability to fly because of a complete lack of ground predators. In adapting to a terrestrial existence, the species has undergone several changes to its structure and appearance.

Most notably, its wings are purely vestigial, similar to those of penguins but far less powerful. Its head is noticeably larger than that of its relatives, while its feet are stronger and more powerful, enabling it to swim more effectively. Despite being so small, the wings are still held out to dry after swimming, for like other members of its family this species does not possess oil-glands with which to waterproof its plumage.

Flightless Cormorants have a distinctive courtship display, involving the male and female walking up and down in a stylised posture to cement the pair bond between them. Unlike many other seabirds they do build a rudimentary nest, decorating it with old rope, bits of plastic, and in one case a dead marine iguana.

The population of Flightless Cormorants is, as you might expect, small – rarely rising above the 1,000 mark. As with other Galápagos birds, numbers fluctuate depending on the availability of food, in particular with the periodic climatic phenomenon 'El Niño'. The increased frequency of El Niño years, in which the region's climate changes dramatically, may yet pose a threat to this unique bird.

The wings of the Flightless Cormorant are held out to dry after swimming

FLIGHTLESS CORMORANT

Phalacrocorax harrisi

As they sail across a clear blue tropical sky, hardly flapping their wings for hours on end, frigatebirds convey an effortless superiority over everything beneath them, humans included. When their interest turns towards food, and they harry some unfortunate tropicbird in order to force it into dropping or regurgitating its catch, their mastery of the air appears complete.

Yet the Magnificent Frigatebird, like the other four members of its family, has one weak link: unable to waterproof its feathers, it must never land on the surface of the sea. If it is forced to do so, it will usually become waterlogged and drown. Explorers, including Christopher Columbus, regarded them as a good omen, because their presence over a ship was supposed to indicate that land was not far away.

In fact frigatebirds are able to fly for long distances over the ocean, because their light skeleton and low wing-loading (the lowest of any bird) enables them to fly effortlessly for days on end without tiring. This is crucial to their survival, as food supplies in the open ocean can be unpredictable, and frigatebirds, like other seabirds, may have to travel hundreds or even thousands of miles away from their breeding colonies in order to find food.

The male frigatebird, with his red gular pouch fully puffed up

The largest of its family, with a body-length of over a metre and a wingspan nudging 2.5 m, the Magnificent Frigatebird is widely distributed on both the Pacific and Atlantic coasts of the Americas, as well as having a tiny, relict population – fewer than a dozen pairs – on the Cape Verde Islands off the coast of West Africa. Threatened by local fishermen, this colony appears to be doomed to extinction.

Like other frigatebirds, this species is a colonial breeder, usually nesting whenever the dry season occurs at its particular location. In one of the bird world's best-known courtship displays, males puff up their red gular pouch until it becomes almost impossibly large and balloon-like, then perform in groups to impress the watching females.

Although females breed every two years, some males in the Caribbean colonies breed every year, taking advantage of the abundant local supplies of food to take a second mate, and thereby doubling their chances of reproductive success. Because the vast majority of pairs only breed every two years, however, the species can be very vulnerable to changes in conditions. The introduction of feral goats and cats has wreaked havoc on some colonies.

The Magnificent Frigatebird is largely sedentary, but individuals do occasionally wander, and vagrants have reached as far afield as Alaska, Denmark and the Isle of Man. Other records of unidentified frigatebirds off Britain and the eastern USA almost certainly refer to this species.

MAGNIFICENT FRIGATEBIRD | *Fregata magnificens*

FRIGATEBIRDS EARNED GRUDGING RESPECT FROM EARLY SAILORS, WHO, OBSERVING THEIR PIRATICAL HABITS, GAVE THEM THEIR POPULAR NAME, 'MAN O'WAR BIRDS'

The characteristic booming of the breeding male Eurasian Bittern is one of the most extraordinary sounds of the bird world. Indeed, it is considered to be the most far-reaching of all bird calls, as it can be heard from a distance of 8 km.

The Bittern creates the sound by stretching its neck, pointing its dagger-shaped bill directly upwards, then emitting the boom from deep within its body cavity. The sound has been likened to someone blowing hard across the neck of a bottle, and it has proved both confusing and frightening to its hearers.

Yet while hearing this reed-dwelling species is relatively straightforward, seeing one is far from simple. The Bittern spends most of its life deep inside the densest part of a reed bed, only occasionally emerging at the edge, where its extraordinary camouflage renders it difficult to see. Bitterns are notoriously reluctant to fly, and usually only do so for a short distance before once again dropping down into their reedy home.

It is hardly surprising, then, that the plethora of folk names for the species derive from its booming sound, including 'bumble', 'butter bump' and 'bull o'the bog'. The Bittern's scientific name, *Botaurus*, commemorates the species' association with bulls.

Despite their reluctance to fly, Bitterns can and do migrate long distances, with juvenile birds having been recorded hundreds of kilometres away from their birthplace. However, because the species is a nocturnal migrant, such movements are rarely if ever observed.

Like so many other wetland species, the Bittern suffered major declines during the 19th and 20th centuries, due to the usual litany of land drainage, water pollution and persecution. Fortunately Bitterns are no longer hunted for food – though they were once a gastronomic treat for medieval kings, served alongside peacocks, cranes and curlews at important events such as coronations.

Today the species is considered 'Near-threatened', especially in Europe, where the total population (excluding Russia) is fewer than 3,000 pairs. Coastal breeding Bitterns, notably those in the low-lying regions of eastern Britain, are currently threatened by the consequences of global climate change. These include a rise in sea levels, which may eventually destroy their breeding areas, and the effect of more frequent storms, which can flood reed beds with salt or brackish water, making them unsuitable for the freshwater Bittern.

On the more positive side, a reduction in the frequency of very cold winters may be good news for a species which is very vulnerable to sudden cold snaps.

Though Bitterns are reluctant to fly, they will do so occasionally

Botaurus stellaris | # EURASIAN BITTERN

LEGEND HAS IT THAT SOLDIERS FROM AN ARMY CROSSING THE EBRO DELTA IN NORTHEAST SPAIN BY NIGHT WERE TERRORISED BY THE SOUND OF BOOMING BITTERNS, AND FLED IN PANIC AS A RESULT

The Old Testament Book of Jeremiah contains one of the earliest references to bird migration: 'Yea, the stork in the heavens knoweth her appointed times.'

The bird in question was undoubtedly the White Stork, a species that still passes through Israel in vast numbers on its twice-yearly journeys to and from its breeding grounds in Europe and western Asia to its winter quarters in sub-Saharan Africa.

The reason storks are seen in such big flocks on migration is that they are large, heavy birds and find it very difficult to cross large expanses of water such as the Mediterranean Sea. Instead they seek out the shortest possible crossings, at Gibraltar in the west, and the Bosporus and Eilat in the east, where together with other large birds such as cranes and eagles they take advantage of thermal air currents to gain enough height to make the narrow sea-crossing.

Because they are so easy to see, scientists have been able to track their movements with a high degree of accuracy, enabling us to learn more about the White Stork's migration than almost any other species.

The name 'stork' apparently derives from the Old German for 'stick', which is a reference to the bird's upright appearance, almost certainly with phallic overtones. This might explain the widely-held (though erroneous!) belief that storks bring babies. Another possible explanation is that migrating storks returned to their northern homes at the start of spring, nine months after midsummer, and, as a result, were regarded as a symbol of fertility.

White Storks are also the subject of many other beliefs and sayings, especially in central and eastern Europe, where it is always considered good luck to have storks nesting on one's roof. But the human inhabitants may end up cursing their neighbours, for nesting White Storks regularly indulge in noisy displays of bill-clattering.

Like so many European wetland birds, White Storks have suffered greatly in recent decades from habitat loss. This, together with the fact that their size makes them an easy target for hunters, has led to the species being categorised as 'Near-threatened'. However, recent conservation efforts, including the widespread provision of platforms on houses for them to nest on, may now be reversing the downward trend.

White Storks are opportunistic feeders, with a marked preference for frogs, snakes and lizards. An old Polish folktale asserts that these animals had been put in a sack by God to rid the world of them, but the man entrusted to dispose of the sack in the sea became curious, opened the sack, and the creatures inside escaped. He was turned into a stork as a punishment, and has been hunting his quarries ever since.

It is considered good luck to have storks nesting on your roof – here they are on the minaret of a mosque in Morocco

Ciconia ciconia | # EUROPEAN WHITE STORK

ODDLY, THE ANCIENT GREEKS BELIEVED THAT THE STORK CARRYING A BABY WAS A SYMBOL OF STEALING IT RATHER THAN BRINGING IT

In 1860, just ten years after the species had first been discovered in the fetid papyrus swamps of East Africa, two Shoebills were brought to London Zoo and put on display. Like the Duck-billed Platypus, people assumed the creature was an elaborate hoax: how could a bird possibly have such an extraordinary, clog-shaped bill?

But the Shoebill is very real indeed. The bird is tall, with a deep blue-grey plumage, and the bill is certainly its most striking feature. About 19 cm long, and almost as wide and deep, it is thought to be an adaptation for feeding in dense aquatic vegetation, where the best way to catch fleeing prey is to plunge its head down with as much speed and force as it can muster. It also uses its bill as a water container, pouring cooling liquid over its chicks to protect them from the sun's heat.

The species lives in the papyrus swamps and marshes of central East Africa, from southern Sudan and Ethiopia in the north to the Congos and Zambia in the south. The reason the Shoebill prefers these stagnant swamps is that with less oxygen present in the water, fish need to come near the surface more frequently, and so are easier to catch.

Like other birds that are the sole representatives of their families, the Shoebill has long puzzled taxonomists. Some consider it a relative of the storks, while more recent studies have indicated that it might share common ancestry with the pelicans – another group with intense and sometimes violent feeding methods!

Shoebills are solitary birds except during the breeding season – and even then males and females often feed at opposite ends of their territory. Their slow, stately movements contrast with the speed of their killing strike. Their solitary habits make them hard to study, and little is known about their true conservation status. However, their fairly local distribution, and a population estimated at between 5,000 and 8,000 individuals, do give some cause for concern.

Like many wetland birds, the Shoebill's habitat is under constant threat from drainage for agriculture to produce food for local and global markets. Another problem is the demand from zoos around the world, which has led to villagers being offered substantial financial rewards for capturing the birds. A single Shoebill can fetch as much as $20,000 (about £10,500).

The Shoebill is a firm favourite with birders. The name was originally given to the species by the 19th-century ornithologist John Gould, who described the Shoebill as 'the most extraordinary bird I have seen for many years'.

The Shoebill, with its extraordinary clog-shaped bill

Balaeniceps rex | # SHOEBILL

THE CALIFORNIA LICENCE PLATE OF THE LATE AMERICAN 'WORLD LISTER' ARNOLD SMALL BORE THE LEGEND 'B. REX' — AN ABBREVIATION OF THE SHOEBILL'S SCIENTIFIC NAME, *BALAENICEPS REX*, MEANING 'KING WHALE-HEAD'

Some birds truly deserve their name, and the Scarlet Ibis is certainly one of them. Apart from its black wingtips, its plumage is a vivid orange-red, almost luminous in quality.

The range of the Scarlet Ibis extends across much of the northern tip of South America, from Colombia and Ecuador, through Venezuela and the Guianas, to the Amazon Delta of Brazil. Their stronghold is the *llanos* of Venezuela and eastern Colombia, a vast, wet grassland plain crisscrossed by the Orinoco River and its tributaries. In this area the ibises are able to feed and breed away from disturbance by humans.

The Scarlet Ibis is also a common non-breeding visitor to Trinidad, where the roost at Caroni Swamp attracts thousands of visitors each year, eager to view the evening spectacle; the bird is even on the itinerary of passing cruise ships.

The bird's fame has led to it being used by American writer James Hurst as the title of a short story. Published in 1960, this classic tale of the relationship between a young boy and his disabled brother has been a staple text of American high-school literature classes ever since.

The Scarlet Ibis is a sociable bird, which, as well as roosting in vast numbers, also feeds in loose flocks of up to 70 birds. Like other members of its family, it uses its long decurved bill to feed in shallow water, using the sensitive tip to locate its crustacean food in the muddy bottoms of its swampy home.

The advantage of communal feeding is that because ibises look downwards when searching for food, they are very vulnerable to predators, so by forming flocks they lessen the risk of attack.

Breeding takes place in colonies – sometimes containing as many as 5,000 pairs – often in the company of other species of waterbird such as herons and egrets. Nests are built from a platform of sticks, and the downy young often fall out of this flimsy structure and end up in a watery grave, where their remains are scavenged by predators such as alligators.

The Scarlet Ibis's closest relative is the American White Ibis, which replaces it to the north of its range in the Caribbean and the southern United States. Amazingly, given their obvious differences in appearance, there is now a proposal to 'lump' the two species into one, based on the many instances in which the two have been known to hybridise.

The colour of the Scarlet Ibis means it truly lives up to its name

SCARLET IBIS | *Eudocimus ruber*

THE SCARLET IBIS IS ONE OF THE MOST CELEBRATED SPECIES IN ITS FAMILY AND IS THE NATIONAL BIRD OF TRINIDAD & TOBAGO

There cannot be many birds that have been put up for election, but the Black-faced Spoonbill is one of them. In Taiwan's presidential contest, held in March 2000, a group of students decided to draw attention to the plight of this endangered species by entering it on the ballot as a 'write-in' candidate. The spoonbill did not actually win, but the resulting publicity helped to safeguard its future in Taiwan.

Because it is relatively easy to see, birders did not become fully aware of the seriousness of the Black-faced Spoonbill's plight until the late 1980s, by which time the world population had fallen to an estimated 288 individuals.

Thanks to emergency conservation measures in its three main wintering areas – coastal China, Hong Kong and Taiwan – numbers have since risen to a total world population estimated at just over 1,400 birds, about two-thirds of which winter in Taiwan.

The history of the Black-faced Spoonbill is typical of so many wetland birds of southeast Asia, whose misfortune is to live in a region undergoing the fastest economic growth in history. To achieve this financial and social miracle, wetlands are being drained; and even if the birds survive, they are suffering the effects of pollution and disturbance.

Though its wintering grounds are well known and are mostly protected, the same

The Black-faced Spoonbill, the smallest of the spoonbill family

cannot be said of its breeding areas. Indeed, the only known colony – comprising just 30 pairs – is in North Korea, with others suspected – but not yet discovered – in northeast China. The species once nested in South Korea, but disturbance and habitat loss during the Korean War in the 1950s drove the spoonbills away.

Today, disturbance on the birds' wintering grounds is another cause for concern, particularly in Hong Kong, where they are often prevented from feeding at low tide by the presence of fishermen gathering shellfish. Nevertheless, Hong Kong is still one of the most accessible places for western birders to see this much-sought-after species.

The Black-faced Spoonbill is the smallest member of the distinctive subfamily of spoonbills, which are considered to share a common ancestor with ibises and are placed in the same family. The other five spoonbills are found in wetland habitats throughout the world: Roseate Spoonbill in the Americas; African Spoonbill in Africa; Royal and Yellow-billed Spoonbills in Australasia; and the best-known, Eurasian Spoonbill, in Europe, Asia and Africa.

All share the same spatulate bill, which they use to feed by sweeping it from side to side in a strategy known as 'tactile foraging' (as opposed to the 'visual foraging' method employed by herons and storks). Sensors within the 'spoon' detect tiny vibrations of their prey, at which the bird snaps its bill shut.

BLACK-FACED SPOONBILL | *Platalea minor*

DESPITE ITS DISAPPEARANCE FROM THE COUNTRY, THE BLACK-FACED SPOONBILL IS STILL RECOGNISED AS A NATIONAL ICON IN SOUTH KOREA

The salt lakes of East Africa's Rift Valley are amongst the most hostile, desolate and barren environments on earth. Yet one species of bird has not only evolved to live there, but its assemblages are the largest known for any non-passerine bird on earth. That bird is the Lesser Flamingo.

As both its English and scientific names suggest, this is the smallest of the six species of flamingo. Even so, it stands almost a metre tall, making it one of the largest waterbirds of the region.

But although it shares the bright salmon-pink plumage and elegant shape of its relatives, the Lesser Flamingo is undoubtedly best viewed at a distance – preferably from the air, where thousands and thousands of individuals coalesce into a single pixellated patch of pink, in stark contrast to the grey-blue waters that surround it.

The Lesser Flamingo has oddly erratic breeding habits: pairs do not breed every year, depending on the availability of food in the area. When they do breed, they form huge colonies – the largest boasting more than one million pairs.

Like all its family, the Lesser Flamingo is a highly specialised feeder. Its diet is almost exclusively made up of microscopic blue-green algae and other microorganisms called diatoms, though it does occasionally feed on larger items such as small invetebrates. Like all flamingos, it feeds by inverting its head so that the top of the bill is partly submerged beneath the surface of the shallow water; then, using its large, fleshy tongue as a pump, it filters the water containing these tiny organisms into its bill.

This may seem a complex solution to the problem of finding food, but it is highly effective: the single flock of flamingos on Kenya's Lake Nakuru has been estimated to consume about 60 tonnes of algae per day.

Perhaps surprisingly for such a long-legged bird, the Lesser Flamingo is adept at swimming – often venturing into quite deep waters in order to exploit an abundant food supply.

The inaccessibility of the flamingos' habitat means that it is rarely troubled by predators, and with a global population estimated at up to six million birds it is not globally threatened. However, the unexplained death of up to 100,000 birds in East Africa during 2006 does give major cause for concern.

For such a striking and beautiful bird, it seems surprising that flamingos of all kinds managed to avoid the same fate as the egrets, which were killed in huge numbers to satisfy the plumage trade in the 19th and early 20th centuries. The clue as to why lies in their diet: the pink hue in flamingos' plumage comes from the carotenoid pigments in the algae on which they feed, and swiftly fades once the bird has been killed.

Thousands of individual Lesser Flamingos create a patch of pink at Lake Naivasha in Kenya

Phoeniconaias minor | # LESSER FLAMINGO

IN ADDITION TO LESSER FLAMINGOS, THE ONLY OTHER ORGANISMS IN THE ANIMAL KINGDOM TO USE SUCH A SPECIALISED METHOD OF FEEDING ARE THE BALEEN WHALES

Thomas Bewick's *British Birds*, published in two volumes at the turn of the 19th century, sold by the thousand, and did more to foster an interest in birds amongst the ordinary reading public than any previous work.

The swan that perpetuates Bewick's fame goes under two other names in North America: Tundra Swan, from its habitat, and Whistling Swan, from its call. The North American race differs noticeably from its Siberian counterpart in that its bill is virtually all black, apart from a tiny sliver of yellow towards the eye, whereas that of the race *bewickii* has broad patches of yellow.

It was Peter (later Sir Peter) Scott, arguably the greatest conservationist of the modern era, who first realised that the pattern of yellow on each bird's bill is in fact unique, making it possible to identify individual Bewick's Swans. For many years, with the help of his artist daughter Dafila, he created an identity guide to the swans visiting his home at the Wildfowl Trust's headquarters at Slimbridge in Gloucestershire.

This allowed him to note the arrival and departure dates of each bird from year to year, which in turn enabled him to work out the pair bonds between males and females. His most famous swan visitor, Lancelot, returned to Slimbridge each winter

The pattern on Bewick's Swans' bills can also be seen in flight

for more than 20 years, bringing three 'wives' with him during that period.

Such advances in our knowledge are incredible when we consider that the very first time a human being cast eyes on the nest and eggs of a Bewick's Swan was less than a century earlier. It was British ornithologist and explorer Henry Seebohm who did so, after a long and arduous journey by train, boat and sledge to the delta of the Pechora River.

Recently, much more has been learned about the breeding and migration of Bewick's Swans, using radio-tracking devices that allow scientists to follow the birds on their migration westwards from their breeding grounds on the Siberian tundra to the Netherlands and Britain.

Once they reach their wintering areas in Europe they are relatively safe – in sharp contrast to North America, where they continue to suffer from illegal hunting and especially poisoning from lead shot, which is also a hazard in Russia and eastern Europe.

The sight of a flock of Bewick's Swans flying across a winter sky may, however, become increasingly rare in Britain and western Europe. Milder winters are allowing increasing numbers of swans to cut short their westward journey and spend the winter around the Baltic Sea. If the climate continues to change, it may spell the end of one Russian saying: 'The swan brings snow on its bill.'

BEWICK'S SWAN | *Cygnus columbianus*

THE MAN COMMEMORATED IN THE NAME OF THIS ARCTIC SPECIES OF SWAN IS RIGHTLY REMEMBERED AS THE MAN WHO FIRST BROUGHT BIRD BOOKS TO A MASS AUDIENCE

What links an action movie starring Gene Hackman with a short story about one of the most charismatic of all North American birds? The fact that both *The Poseidon Adventure* and *The Snow Goose* were written by Paul Gallico, clearly one of the most versatile writers of the 20th century.

Gallico's *The Snow Goose*, first published during the Second World War, remains one of the best-known and best-loved short stories ever written. It has inspired many spin-offs, including several plays and films, and even a 1970s concept album recorded by the progressive rock band Camel.

Each autumn, more than a million Snow Geese head south from their breeding grounds in the far north of the Canadian Arctic, to their winter quarters in the southern states of the USA and northern Mexico.

It is not hard to see why this particular species captures the imagination of birders and non-birders alike: no other species (apart from the exceedingly rare Whooping Crane) can boast the Snow Goose's combination of snow-white plumage and haunting call. Add to this the fact that the birds travel in vast flocks, stopping off at favourite 'pitstops' in order to refuel, and their fame is hardly surprising.

After journeying several thousand kilometres, tens of thousands of Snow Geese finally end up at the Bosque del Apache wildlife refuge in New Mexico. As they wheel around the sky in flocks it is one of the most impressive bird spectacles in the world.

Despite the purity of its appearance, the Snow Goose is far from clear from a taxonomic point of view. Historically two distinct races have been recognised: the 'Lesser' Snow Goose, which breeds from Wrangel Island (off northeastern Russia) through Alaska to Baffin Island, and the 'Greater' Snow Goose, which breeds in northwest Greenland and on various islands in Baffin Bay. To further confuse the issue, some birds have a much darker, bluish-grey, plumage, and are colloquially known as the 'Blue' Snow Goose.

Despite the loss of wetland habitat across North America, the Snow Goose is still a very common bird; indeed, the population has more than doubled since the 1960s, almost certainly due to more rigorous control of hunting. However, as one of the commonest Arctic breeding birds its future is not wholly secure, given the possible effects resulting from global climate change, which could threaten the Snow Goose's breeding habitat.

Camouflaged against the snow, a Snow Goose at Klamath Basin in California

Anser (Chen) caerulescens | # SNOW GOOSE

THE SNOW GOOSE INSPIRES ARTISTS, WRITERS AND ORDINARY PEOPLE, PARTICULARLY THOSE FORTUNATE ENOUGH TO WITNESS ITS CELEBRATED MIGRATIONS ACROSS THE NORTH AMERICAN CONTINENT

This delicate little goose, barely the size of a Mallard, is arguably the most beautiful of all its family. It is also one of the rarest, with numbers fluctuating from year to year, but rarely rising above 60,000 birds. Its closest relatives are two other small geese in the genus *Branta*, the Barnacle and Brent Geese.

The breeding areas of the Red-breasted Goose lie mainly within the Taimyr Peninsula, a remote tundra region in northern Siberia. Like so many northern breeders, it takes advantage of the brief window of opportunity provided by the Arctic summer, where long daylight hours lead to a surfeit of food, enabling the birds to raise a family. Red-breasted Geese are almost exclusively vegetarian, feeding on the leaves and stems of plants, though in winter they also feed on seeds and grains.

During the winter months, the vast majority of Red-breasted Geese can be found in the Black Sea region of eastern Europe, with more than four-fifths of the world population wintering at just five sites in Bulgaria and Romania.

With such a limited range the species is especially vulnerable to disturbance and habitat loss. Now that its two primary host countries are joining the European Community, many people fear that this process will accelerate. This will be the case especially if the planting of wheat becomes more widespread in the region, leading to a loss of habitat for the geese.

A decline in the Red-breasted Goose population from the middle of the 20th century mirrored a similar decline in raptor species such as Snowy Owl, Peregrine and Rough-legged Buzzard, due to poisoning by agricultural pesticides. The reason for this apparent anomaly was that Red-breasted Geese deliberately breed close to the nests of these predators, as this protects them against attack from their main enemy, the Arctic Fox, and also against the attentions of marauding skuas. In return, the geese provide an early-warning system against intruding foxes.

Now that these raptors are once again on the increase, it is hoped that the geese will enjoy a similar population boom. However, in their wintering areas they are also vulnerable to hunting, especially in Russia and Ukraine, where there is a profitable shooting industry.

In the distant past it may have enjoyed a wider distribution than today: bizarrely, images easily recognisable as Red-breasted Geese appear on the tombs of Ancient Egypt. The most celebrated of these are the famous 'geese of Meidum', now in the Egyptian Museum in Cairo, which date back to the reign of Nefermaat, founder of the 4th Dynasty, about 2,600 years before the birth of Christ. These beautifully preserved paintings have been described as the world's first ornithological record.

A pair of Red-breasted Geese giving a threat display

Branta ruficollis | # RED-BREASTED GOOSE

THE RED-BREASTED GOOSE IS PRONE TO VAGRANCY, REGULARLY JOINING FLOCKS OF BRENT OR WHITE-FRONTED GEESE. BIRDS WANDER OFTEN TO THE NETHERLANDS, AND ON OCCASIONS EVEN CROSS THE NORTH SEA TO BRITAIN AND IRELAND

Once found in virtually every home, the eiderdown is rapidly becoming obsolete as more modern forms of bedding take its place. This clearly causes confusion to some younger people, as can be seen from the following anecdote. Apparently a little boy, visiting the Farne Islands off England's northeast coast for the very first time, caught sight of what he realised was a familiar waterbird. He tugged excitedly at his parents' sleeves, yelling: 'Look, mummy, look daddy – there's a duvet duck!'

Despite the decline of the traditional eiderdown, the soft downy feathers used by the Eider duck to line her nest are still very much in demand. The down, which the female plucks from her own breast in order to keep her eggs and chicks warm, has extraordinary thermal properties.

At the peak of Iceland's eiderdown trade, in the early 20th century, 4,300 kg of down were collected each year from 280,000 female Eiders – on average just over 15 g from each bird. Iceland still exports 2,500 kg every year, more than two-thirds of it going to Japan, where the raw down retails at $600 (£320) per kilo and a luxury eiderdown quilt costs more than $11,000 (about £5,800).

The Common Eider has one other major claim to fame: it was the first species known to have been given official protection, back in the 7th century AD. It was the Bishop of Lindisfarne, St Cuthbert, who decreed that the Eider was to be protected – not quite the act of altruism it may at first seem, as he and his fellow monks made a good living selling the down. As a result, however, the species is still known as Cuthbert's Duck, or Cuddy's Duck, in parts of northeast England.

The Common Eider has a broadly Holarctic distribution, breeding from Alaska and Canada across southern Greenland, northern Europe (south to the British Isles and western France) and Siberia to the Bering Strait. Throughout its range it is usually the commonest species of sea duck. They spend the winter further south, often at sea, where they may be vulnerable to stormy weather or major oil spills.

After breeding, the young gather under the protection of a group of females, in the avian equivalent of a crèche. Meanwhile, the males stand around on rocks moulting, occasionally uttering their extraordinary call, which sounds like a woman of a certain age caught by surprise. Despite their rather lazy reputation, however, Eiders are extremely fast flyers, holding the speed record as the fastest bird recorded in level flight – at an incredible 76.5 km per hour.

An adult male Common Eider in flight in Iceland – one of the world's fastest-flying birds

COMMON EIDER | *Somateria mollissima*

WEIGHT FOR WEIGHT, EIDER DOWN INSULATES BETTER THAN VIRTUALLY ANY OTHER MATERIAL – NATURAL OR MAN-MADE

The decline, fall and resurrection of North America's largest flying bird is both a sorry tale and a parable on the paradox that is modern America. Only in the richest state in the USA (if California were a sovereign nation it would be the fifth richest country in the world) could a species be snatched from the jaws of death by the controversial use of science – plus, of course, many millions of dollars.

In prehistoric times, the California Condor was found across much of North America, in a wide range of habitats, where it hunted alongside the Woolly Mammoth and Sabre-toothed Tiger – and outlived them.

But as the West was won, so this huge, distinctive raptor went into a serious decline. Early explorers Lewis and Clark noted them throughout the north-west, but by the early 1950s there were only an estimated 60 birds remaining in the wild, all in one small region of southern California. The fall in numbers continued inexorably: at its lowest ebb, in 1982, there were just 21 birds alive in the wild.

Drastic action had to be taken, and it finally was. In 1987, all remaining wild California Condors were caught and taken into captivity. Even their very last stronghold, the wooded hills to the north of the city of Los Angeles, no longer sounded to their haunting cry.

The cynics considered the captive-breeding programme to be a vain hope; the idealists were equally condemnatory of what they saw as an assault on the rights of a wild bird to disappear with dignity.

But ultimately both sides were proved wrong. The captive-breeding was a great success, with the first release of 15 birds occurring in 1992, five years after the last wild condors had been captured. The first released birds bred in the wild in 2002 – more than 18 years after the previous successful attempt. The current population stands at about 270, more than 100 of which are flying free in northern and southern California and Arizona's Grand Canyon.

The California Condor does not have particularly specialised habitat requirements, so with luck the new population should do well. Unfortunately, though, many of the threats which led to its original demise are still present. These include shooting, poisoning (from both lead bullets and poisoned animal carcasses) and collisions with power lines – a particular danger to a bird with a wingspan approaching 3 m, and weighing up to 8.5 kg. Sharing its range with almost 40 million people is also occasionally bound to bring the bird into conflict with humans.

But if it can avoid these many hazards and problems, there is a sporting chance that the California Condor may yet defy extinction, and continue to soar across the skies of the world's most powerful nation for centuries to come.

The uplifting sight of North America's largest flying bird

Gymnogyps californianus | # CALIFORNIA CONDOR

NOWHERE ELSE COULD A SPECIES THAT SYMBOLISES THE GO-GETTING, FRONTIER MENTALITY OF ITS HOMELAND BE ALLOWED TO REACH THE VERGE OF EXTINCTION

The Bald Eagle's pre-eminence as America's national bird was once threatened by, of all creatures, the Wild Turkey.

As the founding fathers debated the issue at the Second Continental Congress in 1782, Benjamin Franklin made an impassioned plea for the Wild Turkey to be adopted as the symbol of the fledgling state, in preference to the mighty eagle. His reason? The apparently 'poor moral character' of the Bald Eagle.

Since that close call, the Bald Eagle has become the living embodiment of the United States, appearing everywhere from advertising hoardings to bank notes. These use the eagle's perceived strength and character either to sell a product or to endorse it as being quintessentially American. The bird also famously appears on the Presidential Seal.

Mankind's fascination with the Bald Eagle goes back much further. Eagles feature prominently in the myths and legends of the Native Americans: they were said to deliver people from famine, embody the souls of dead warriors, and create thunder and lightning.

Eagles were also a symbol of fertility – not surprisingly, given their huge and very visible nests. Indeed, the Bald Eagle's nest is the largest tree nest of any single bird in the world. Added to each year, one nest in Florida eventually measured 6 m deep by 3 m across, and weighed almost three tonnes – equivalent to the weight of three army jeeps.

Bald Eagles are mainly fish-eaters: hence their abundance on the salmon rivers of Canada and Alaska. Their prey is seized using their huge talons, and they are able to carry fish weighing up to 3.5 kg, up to half their own body-weight.

Like so many of the world's large raptors, Bald Eagles have had a rough ride over the past couple of centuries. Once abundant across the whole of North America, the arrival of Europeans with shotguns led to a rapid decline. This was compounded by the widespread use of agricultural pesticides such as DDT during the 20th century. Hunting was also an issue. Bounties offered by the Alaskan authorities led to the slaughter of up to 150,000 eagles, with the bird's habit of gathering in large flocks to feed making them an easy target.

Whatever the reasons for the Bald Eagle's decline, by the 1950s numbers in the continental United States had fallen to 10,000 pairs. By the 1960s, things were much worse, with fewer than 500 pairs surviving. With the country's national symbol under threat, legislation and protective measures were rushed through Congress, and a slow but steady recovery began. Today the Bald Eagle population in the lower 48 states is estimated to be more than 6,500 breeding pairs. The Bald Eagle is finally being removed from the official list of endangered species.

A Bald Eagle dives for fish in Alaska

Haliaeetus leucocephalus | # BALD EAGLE

BALD EAGLES HAVE BEEN KNOWN TO BREED ON SUBURBAN HOUSING ESTATES, LEADING NERVOUS HOUSEHOLDERS TO KEEP A CLOSE EYE OUT FOR THEIR CATS – AND CHILDREN!

Legend has it that the Ancient Greek playwright Aeschylus was killed when a passing eagle dropped a tortoise on his head, cracking his skull. However, modern ornithologists believe that the so-called 'eagle' was in fact a Lammergeier. The reason they can be so confident of the bird's identity is that this species of vulture feeds almost exclusively on bones, which it drops from great heights to crack them, so it can feed on the nourishing bone marrow within.

Persistence is the key to the Lammergeier's feeding regime: on occasions a bird may have to drop the same bone as many as 50 times before it finally breaks open – each time flying up to 80 m above the ground in order to do so.

Lammergeiers are found in mountainous regions of southern Europe, Asia and Africa, though they are thinly distributed throughout their range. Like most large birds of prey, they have an enormous home territory, sometimes covering thousands of square kilometres.

The English name derives from the German, meaning 'lamb vulture', after their preferred prey. An ancient name is 'ossifrage', meaning 'bone crusher', while some modern ornithologists prefer the name Bearded Vulture, from the bird's small tuft of feathers beneath the lower mandible of the bill.

Even from a distance the unique silhouette renders a Lammergeier unmistakable: with its diamond-shaped tail and long, narrow wings, it looks more like a giant falcon than a vulture. These narrow wings make it much better adapted to gliding than eagles and other vultures, as they provide better lift than broader ones.

The Lammergeier also differs from other vultures in having extensive feathering on its head and neck, a result of the fact that it rarely needs to poke its head into carcasses in order to feed. On the ground, the bird's striking plumage becomes apparent: its dark back and wings and its facial mask contrasting with the rich orange head and underparts.

The Lammergeier's wide global range, extending from the Spanish Pyrenees in the west to China in the east, and from Europe south to the Cape region of South Africa, means that this species is not considered to be globally threatened. In recent years Lammergeiers have been successfully reintroduced to the Alps, where at one time they became extinct due to a combination of shooting, nest-robbing and the widespread use of poisoned baits to trap mammals such as bears. Their return has been helped by the provision of artificial feeding stations, the Lammergeier equivalent of a giant bird-table.

The distinctive silhouette of a Lammergeier in flight

LAMMERGEIER | *Gypaetus barbatus*

LAMMERGEIERS BREED AT ALTITUDES OF UP TO 4,400 M IN INDIA AND PAKISTAN, WHILE BIRDS HAVE BEEN OBSERVED AT HEIGHTS OF MORE THAN 8,000 M IN THE HIMALAYAS, MAKING THEM ONE OF THE WORLD'S HIGHEST-FLYING BIRDS

Until his mid-thirties, George Montagu led a boringly conventional life. Married with six children, lieutenant-colonel of the Wiltshire county militia, and pillar of the community, he could hardly want for more. Yet all he really wanted to do was to spend his life watching birds.

Then, as a result of an extraordinary series of events, he got his wish. In the final decade of the 18th century, following a scandalous love affair, he was court-martialled and forced to resign his commission. At the same time, he fell out with his sons. Making the best of a bad job, he and his new wife Eliza Dorville headed westwards to Kingsbridge in Devon, where he devoted the rest of his life to the study and classification of birds.

Amongst the many species named and classified by Montagu was the smallest of the four European species of harrier, the species that today bears his name. Because of its marked similarity to the larger Hen Harrier, with both the male and female of the two species easily confused, it was one of the last British birds to be classified.

Following standard convention, Montagu did not name the bird after himself, but instead preferred 'Ash-coloured Falcon' – an indication of the superficial similarity between this slender bird and the unrelated family of falcons. Later, two continental ornithologists named the bird Le Busard Montagu, translated into English as Montagu's Harrier.

Montagu's Harrier has a delicately marked plumage, mainly grey with brown markings in the male, brown with a narrow white rump in the female. The breeding range extends from Britain in the northwest, throughout the central and southern parts of Europe, east into Russia and Kazakhstan. The species has two main wintering areas: the western population travels to sub-Saharan Africa, while most eastern birds head to India and Sri Lanka.

Although today it is Britain's rarest breeding bird of prey, Montagu's Harrier is not globally threatened. However, habitat loss due to modern farming methods, along with continued persecution, means that the world population is declining. The chicks in particular are threatened by early harvesting, as the species predominantly nests in cereal crops.

Like other harriers, Montagu's indulge in a courtship ritual known as 'food-passing'. When the male returns to the nest with his prey, instead of bringing it straight in to the female he flies around above her. Usually she will then leave the nest and fly up towards the male, whereupon he drops the food item for her to catch, in a spectacular and impressive display that strengthens their pair bond.

Montagu's Harrier has long, slender wings and a delicately marked plumage

Circus pygargus | # MONTAGU'S HARRIER

MONTAGU'S HARRIER IS ONE OF THE MOST BEAUTIFUL OF ALL BIRDS OF PREY, WITH A BUOYANT FLIGHT ON LONG, SLENDER WINGS

Named after the winged monsters of Ancient Greek myth, which had the head of a woman and the wings of a bird, this South and Central American raptor is a true giant. At up to 105 cm long, and with females weighing as much as 9 kg – twice as much as their partners – this is the largest and heaviest of the world's two-dozen or so species of true eagle.

The Harpy Eagle is also one of the most beautiful of the world's large raptors. Its plumage shows a dramatic contrast between mostly white underparts and all-dark upperparts, with a grey head, a noticeable crest and – one of its most striking features – a huge, thick-set bill.

This species hunts by cruising low over the forest edge or across the tree canopy, keeping its eyes and ears open in order to locate its quarry. Using its fearsome talons, the Harpy Eagle preys on large mammals, including Capuchin and Howler Monkeys, porcupines and even domestic pigs. It also sometimes hunts reptiles, including large snakes. Sloths form up to a third of the eagle's prey, mainly because their habit of clinging to treetops in the early morning to warm up makes them easy to pick off! The largest prey item known to have been taken by a Harpy Eagle was a Howler Monkey, estimated at 7 kg – about three-quarters of the bird's weight.

Like many very large birds, this eagle breeds only once every two or three years. The two eggs are incubated for about 56 days, though the second chick to be born invariably dies as it fails to compete with its older and larger sibling. This phenomenon, common in many large birds of prey, is known as the 'Cain and Abel syndrome', after the Bible story of the brothers in the Book of Genesis. The surviving youngster will remain in the nest for a further four-and-a-half months, before continuing to be fed by both parents for a year or more afterwards, until it is able to hunt for itself.

The Harpy Eagle has a wide but patchy distribution. It is found across much of tropical Central and South America: from Guatemala and Panama south to Paraguay, southern Brazil and northeastern Argentina.

Its extraordinary appearance and huge size have led to the Harpy Eagle being named the national bird of Panama, although there, as in so much of the region, it has declined as a result of habitat loss and hunting. In fact persecution is the greatest threat to the species: as it hunts mainly along woodland edges it can cope with deforestation, but its low flight and huge size make it an easy target for the shotgun.

The majestic Harpy Eagle is the national bird of Panama

HARPY EAGLE | *Harpia harpyja*

STORIES OF THE HARPY EAGLE MAKING OFF WITH INFANT HUMANS ARE, LIKE THOSE TOLD ABOUT OTHER SPECIES OF EAGLE ELSEWHERE IN THE WORLD, PURE MYTH

The Secretary Bird is much admired by people throughout sub-Saharan Africa, both for its distinctively upright, haughty stance and for its impressive ability to kill snakes with a single blow. The name is usually thought to come from the feathers behind the ears, which closely resemble the quill pens used by medieval 'secretaries' (the equivalent of modern book-keepers). However, it has also been suggested that the name derives from an Arabic phrase meaning 'hunter-bird' – appropriate given the species' impressive ability to track down and catch its prey.

As with other species which are the only representatives of their families, this peculiar-looking bird has been the subject of much dispute amongst the taxonomists. In the past it has been suggested that the Secretary Bird is closest in evolutionary terms to cranes, or even bustards. Yet although it behaves very like a stork, hunting on foot, it is now considered to be most closely related to the eagles, with which it shares a similar skeletal structure.

The Secretary Bird stands over 1.2 m tall on its enormously long legs, giving it a very good view over the African savannah and open grassland that is its home. Always on the lookout for danger, it can take to the air in a single bound if threatened with attack, flying away on long, narrow wings, its legs trailing behind.

Those legs are also essential for hunting: the Secretary Bird catches its prey by hunting it down visually with its acute eyesight, and then stamping on it. Its powerful feet can make short work of prey as small as a moth, through lizards and snakes, to hares – though its preferred food consists mostly of grasshoppers and locusts.

Having been dispatched quickly and efficiently, the prey is swallowed whole. Some birds have mistaken golf balls for eggs and made an unfortunate dietary error as a result. Another hazard is piracy: having done all the hard work and caught its prey, a Secretary Bird may be unlucky enough to have its meal stolen by a rapacious Tawny Eagle.

Like many African grassland and savannah species, the Secretary Bird has a very wide range, from Senegal in the west to Somalia in the east, and all the way down to South Africa. In Sudan it is the national bird, and appears in the centre of the Presidential Flag, holding a banner reading 'Victory is Ours'.

The Secretary Bird holding its prey, and clearly displaying the feathers behind the ears

Sagittarius serpentarius | # SECRETARY BIRD

DESPITE THEIR LARGELY TERRESTRIAL LIFESTYLE, SECRETARY BIRDS TAKE TO THE AIR TO PERFORM THEIR BIZARRE COURTSHIP DISPLAY, IN WHICH MALE AND FEMALE SOAR HIGH IN THE SKY ON OUTSTRETCHED WINGS, UTTERING THEIR GUTTURAL CALL

The title of the fastest living creature on earth is not easily won, but the Peregrine beats all-comers to this record. No other bird can match its speed, achieved when the Peregrine enters a 'stoop', plummeting towards its prey in order to take advantage of speed and surprise. During this brief plunge, Peregrines have been have been said to reach speeds of up to 300 km per hour, though a more usual speed would be closer to 180 km per hour. Whatever the true figure, it is still breathtaking to watch.

Peregrines are amongst the world's most cosmopolitan and widespread birds, rivalled only by the Barn Owl, Cattle Egret and Osprey in their ability to colonise the world's major land masses. They are found from the polar regions of Greenland and Siberia to the deserts of North Africa, and from Tierra del Fuego to Alaska. As a result, the species has diverged into at least 19 races, some of which – notably the Barbary Falcon of North Africa and the Middle East – are often considered to be separate species. Some of these races are now very rare, being confined to limited areas such as the Cape Verde Islands off the west coast of Africa.

In most parts of their range their preferred food is pigeon, but Peregrines use their hunting technique to catch a variety of airborne prey. They are opportunistic feeders, and have been known to take many other species of bird, as well as bats and even large insects. Their preference for pigeons has got them into trouble, especially in Britain, where pigeon racing is a popular sport. Now that Peregrines have largely recovered from their population collapse of the 1950s and 1960s, and have moved into many towns and cities, the clash between the two cultures of pigeon-racers and birders is becoming a serious issue.

A Peregrine plunging after a Kittiwake on an English coastal cliff

The original decline of the Peregrine – both in Europe and in North America – was the result of two major factors: first, the shooting of Peregrines during World War II, when they were seen as a threat to pigeons carrying military messages; and second, the widespread use and abuse of agricultural pesticides, most notoriously DDT, in the years after the war. Eventually, study of breeding falcons revealed that the accumulation of DDT in this top predator was affecting the thickness of their eggshells, and therefore dramatically reducing breeding success. This revelation, in Rachel Carson's seminal book *Silent Spring*, came just in time to save the Peregrine in Britain and the USA, where numbers had reached critically low levels.

To see one of these magnificent birds soaring over the urban skyline, using the structure of our cities as the perfect substitute for more natural habitats, fills the heart of anyone – apart from pigeon fanciers – with joy.

PEREGRINE | *Falco peregrinus*

TODAY, PEREGRINES ARE BACK WHERE THEY BELONG, IN A VARIETY OF URBAN AND RURAL HABITATS THROUGHOUT THE WORLD.

The Malleefowl of Australia boasts one of the most extraordinary forms of breeding behaviour of any bird – a distinction shared with the other 18 members of its family, the megapodes.

For the Malleefowl and its close relatives are the only birds in the world whose eggs are not incubated by an adult bird. Instead, they build an enormous mound out of vegetation, lay their eggs inside and leave them, allowing the heat generated by the rotting vegetable matter to incubate them. Along with the offspring of the various species of brood parasites such as cuckoos and cowbirds, the young Malleefowl has the unusual distinction of never knowingly meeting its parents. Because it gets no help, the young needs to be able to burrow out of its mound and feed itself as soon as it is born. As a result, the chicks of all megapodes are the most precocial – advanced – of any bird.

Even by the standards of the megapode family, the Malleefowl has some notable distinctions. Most other megapodes live in dense tropical forest, mainly in the islands north of Australia such as New Guinea, Vanuatu and Sulawesi, where they are notoriously difficult to see. The Malleefowl, in contrast, lives in more open woodland and scrub. It also has a more southerly, warm-temperate distribution, ranging from Western Australia, through South Australia, to parts of Victoria and New South Wales. Further, while the other members of its family are a rather uniform dark brown, chestnut or grey in colour, the Malleefowl has a delicately marked plumage with scalloped feather edgings.

One probable reason why the Malleefowl lives in more open habitats is that it cannot rely entirely on the heat produced by the fermenting vegetation to incubate its eggs; so by nesting in more exposed places it takes advantage of the warmth of the sun's rays – the only megapode to do so.

Sadly the Malleefowl has suffered badly from the attentions of hunters (the bird is large and plump), egg-harvesting and loss of habitat, as Australia's growing human population takes over more and more land for agriculture, fragmenting the species' habitat. Bushfires are also a major concern, especially as global warming appears to be leading to a greater incidence of fires, with less time for the habitat to recover between each event.

Today, the Malleefowl population is estimated at well below 10,000 pairs, and the species is classified as 'Vulnerable', though a recovery programme, including captive-breeding, is under way. Ironically, a closely related species, the Australian Brush-turkey, has expanded its range in the past few decades, and is now causing problems in suburban Brisbane gardens by building its huge mounds on top of people's prize flowerbeds!

A male Malleefowl on his nest mound, in which the eggs will be laid

MALLEEFOWL | *Leipoa ocellata*

THE MALLEEFOWL'S NAME DERIVES FROM 'MALLEE', A DWARF FORM OF EUCALYPTUS

Dawn in the Caledonian pine forest of northern Scotland brings with it an extraordinary sound. Even before the first rays of light filter through to the forest floor, through the trees comes a sound best described as like hearing a bottle of champagne being opened – in reverse! In this case, the peculiar series of glugging notes is followed by a loud 'pop'.

The sound comes from a male Capercaillie, in the process of displaying to rival males and apparently uninterested females, in a lek. Lekking is a bizarre form of courtship behaviour that has evolved – quite independently it seems – in a small number but across a broad range of species, including grouse, waders, manakins and birds-of-paradise. It even occurs in some mammals, including walruses and fruit bats.

Lekking occurs when there is a plentiful supply of food, so that males do not have to devote time and energy to defending territories and finding food for their young. Instead, they dedicate even more time, and excessive amounts of energy, to performing on what can only be described as a stage.

Capercaillies generally begin lekking early in the year, and continue throughout the breeding season. The display is largely performed to impress other males, though a passing female will stop to examine her potential mate.

The Capercaillie is the largest member of the grouse family – at up to 6.5 kg, males are typically at least twice, sometimes three times, as heavy as the females – and can be found in mature conifer forests in a belt across northern Europe from Scotland and Scandinavia through to central Asia. In eastern Asia it is replaced by the closely related Black-billed Capercaillie.

With a global population numbering in the low millions, the species is not threatened, though locally it suffers from hunting, disturbance and the effects of wetter springs, a possible result of global climate change. In Scotland, measures taken to reduce deer problems, such as fences to keep them out of forests, have led to many Capercaillie deaths, as they fly low and fast.

Not surprisingly, being such a large and impressive bird, the Capercaillie has received its fair share of attention, even having a Scottish folk band named after it. The name itself derives, apparently, from a Gaelic phrase meaning 'horse of the woods', presumably a reference to that extraordinary call. This name took some time to become popular, with English naturalists preferring the less evocative name 'Wood Grouse' until the mid-19th century, when the Scottish name finally gained ascendancy.

The remarkable sight of a male Capercaillie displaying and calling

Tetrao urogallus | # WESTERN CAPERCAILLIE

OCCASIONALLY A MALE CAPERCAILLIE WILL GET SO FIRED UP THAT HE WILL APPROACH OTHER CREATURES – INCLUDING PEOPLE – AND DISPLAY TO THEM

The pheasants of the Himalayan foothills boast a unique combination of striking beauty and extreme elusiveness. Few more so than the Satyr Tragopan, a near-mythical creature named after a genuinely mythical one. In Greek mythology, satyrs were half-man, half-goat, and they roamed the woods and mountains in the company of Pan and Dionysus. They were celebrated for their priapic male sexuality, although the bird named after them is no more promiscuous than any other member of the pheasant family.

Another, Hindu, myth says that a god took the most beautiful feather from all known birds and created a new one – the tragopan. Whatever the truth, he appears to have succeeded.

All five species of tragopan are found in the mid-to-high-altitude forests of southeast Asia, from north Pakistan to southeast China. The range of the Satyr Tragopan stretches west to east across the Himalayan mountain range, from northern India through Nepal, Sikkim and Bhutan to southeast Tibet.

The species is generally found at an altitude of between 2,400 and 4,250 m, and requires primary forest, usually of oak and rhododendron, with a dense understorey enabling the birds to avoid detection by predators. In winter they will move down to lower levels, around 2,100 m. As a result of the remoteness and

The stunning beauty of the Satyr Tragopan

inaccessibility of their home, Satyr Tragopans are notoriously hard to see.

Like its close relatives, Blyth's and Temminck's Tragopans, the male Satyr Tragopan boasts a rich, deep red plumage. Closer examination reveals delicate white spots, edged with brown, known as *ocelli* (Italian for 'little eyes'), which cover much of the bird's back and underparts. Along with other members of its family it has long lappets – extraordinary facial flaps which it uses, along with two prominent horns, when displaying to its mate. This feature has given tragopans their alternative name of 'Horned Pheasants'.

Male Satyr Tragopans have an extraordinary wailing call, usually issued at dawn between April and June, as the breeding season gets under way. After mating, the birds build a crude nest out of sticks, high in the branches of a tree, and lay two or three eggs, after which the male may abandon the female and seek out a second mate.

Although not officially classified as under threat, the loss of the tragopan's forest habitat, especially through extensive logging for fuel and timber, does give some cause for concern. Fortunately conservation programmes are now in place, and the Satyr Tragopan may yet turn out to be instrumental in safeguarding the future of its home – as its mysterious habits and beautiful plumage make it ideal for adoption as a 'flagship species' for its threatened mountain habitat.

SATYR TRAGOPAN | *Tragopan satyra*

THE SATYR TRAGOPAN IS ONE OF THE MOST STUNNINGLY BEAUTIFUL BIRDS IN THE WORLD. THE NAME 'TRAGOPAN' COMES FROM THE GREEK *TRAGOS* (GOAT) AND THE HALF-GOAT DEITY PAN

The discovery, in the mid-1930s, of an entirely new species of pheasant living in central Africa was remarkable for two reasons. First, that a member of this family should be found in this vast continent at all – all the other 50 or so species of pheasant originated in Asia, and apart from deliberate introductions into Europe and North America, still live there. Second, because of the extraordinary circumstances of its discovery.

The story goes back to more than 20 years earlier, to 1913, when American ornithologist James Chapin met an inhabitant of a Congolese forest who was wearing an unusual feather in his hat, which he was unable to identify. Later, in 1936, Chapin was visiting a museum in the city of Tervuren in Belgium when he noticed a pair of birds described as 'Indian Blue Peafowl'. Recognising the wing feather as being the same as the one he had collected so many years before, Chapin realised that he was looking at an entirely new species, later named Congo Peafowl.

The elusiveness of the bird itself – together with the extremely dangerous nature of the region in which it lives – means sightings are unfortunately few and far between. The knowledge we have is gleaned mostly from captive-bred birds in Antwerp and Jersey Zoos and various other institutions.

In a wild state, the Congo Peafowl lives in the primary forest on either side of the Congo River. Local people are known to trap the bird for food, but almost constant warfare in the region means that few ornithologists have been able to venture into its breeding areas in recent years. Indeed, we know so little about the bird that until recently BirdLife International was unable to assign a category of threat to the species, simply describing it as 'insufficiently known'. After extensive surveys failed to find the bird across much of its range, it has now been reclassified as 'Threatened', with a population that is estimated at between 2,500 and 10,000 individuals.

Compared to its more famous and widespread relative, the Indian Peafowl, the Congo Peafowl is rather less impressive. Much smaller, it has blue-black underparts, dark green upperparts, a prominent black-and-white crown and a red throat.

The threats faced by this unique species are many and increasing. They include habitat loss due to mining, subsistence agriculture and timber logging and, most recently, the human fallout from warfare, including thousands of refugees from Rwanda; and hunting, as peafowl are often captured accidentally in traps set for mammals such as antelope. The only hope lies in the fact that some of the birds live in designated National Parks, where they gain at least a degree of protection.

A male Congo Peafowl – the only pheasant living in Africa

CONGO PEAFOWL | *Afropavo congensis*

IN THE 70 YEARS SINCE ITS DISCOVERY, FEW PEOPLE HAVE BEEN FORTUNATE ENOUGH TO SEE CONGO PEAFOWL IN THE WILD

In a world of truly remarkable birds, the Hoatzin is even more extraordinary than most. It is the only bird in the world to exist entirely on a diet of leaves, the only bird to have claws on its wings, and the only bird to merit not only its own family but its own unique, single-species order, the *Opisthocomiformes*.

Not surprisingly, the taxonomic history of the Hoatzin has been complicated and at times controversial. In the past it has been placed alongside the gamebirds and cranes, but today most scientists put it much further along the evolutionary lineage of birds, somewhere between parrots and turacos.

Adult Hoatzins are beautiful birds: their rich chestnut plumage, bright blue face-patch and yellow underparts, together with their ornate headdress, have earned them the nickname 'Cigana', meaning gypsy. They also have some peculiar habits, including a highly effective form of bathing: they simply wait for a rainstorm and spread their wings; once the rain stops, they climb to the top of the tree canopy and sunbathe until their wings have dried out.

The Hoatzin chick is even more bizarre than its parent. Young Hoatzins have evolved unique claw-like appendages on their wings, with which they clamber about the branches of trees. If approached by an arboreal predator, however, they will deliberately drop into the water and swim to safety.

Hoatzins live in the northern part of South America, to the east of the Andes, mainly in the river basins of the Amazon and Orinoco. Their preferred habitat is large trees alongside rivers, where they sit and feed. Their staple diet of leaves is disdained by most birds, partly because of the difficulties of consuming enough to survive, and partly because they are so hard to digest.

To make the process easier, the Hoatzin crushes the leaves in its crop before beginning more conventional digestion. As a result of its diet, the Hoatzin has a reputation for being rather smelly; in Guyana it is known as the 'stinking pheasant'. Not put off by this, scientists have considered whether they might be able to isolate the bacteria and enzymes in a Hoatzin's gut and transfer them to domestic grazing animals, thus enabling them to digest a wider range of foods.

At present the Hoatzin is not considered to be threatened with extinction. However, the rapid conversion of much of their forest habitat into farmland has already fragmented their original range, and does cast a cloud over their future; especially as the adaptations they have made – to a diet of leaves – mean that they are highly sedentary.

The extraordinary Hoatzin in flight in Venezuela

Opisthocomus hoazin | # HOATZIN

THE HOATZIN'S SCIENTIFIC NAME DERIVES FROM A GREEK PHRASE MEANING 'WEARING LONG HAIR BEHIND', A REFERENCE TO THE PUNK-LIKE CREST SPROUTING FROM THE TOP OF ITS CROWN

The tallest North American bird – at over 1.5 m – is also one of the rarest, despite being brought back from the very brink of extinction. With its pure white plumage, relieved only by black, red and grey head markings, and black wingtips (visible in flight), it is also undoubtedly one of the most beautiful.

Once widespread across the plains and wetlands of North America, the Whooping Crane was – like so many other large, showy birds – a victim of the combination of hunting for food and habitat loss, as the marshy areas on which it depended were drained and converted to intensive agriculture.

By 1941, as the Japanese attacked Pearl Harbour, the entire Whooping Crane population had fallen to crisis level, with just 16 birds alive in the wild. Despite having more urgent matters on their minds, North Americans managed to join forces in a campaign spearheaded by people living along the cranes' migration route, from western Canada to Texas. They came together to form the 'Whooper Club', and persistently lobbied government organisations about the birds' plight.

Today the Whooping Cranes' main breeding grounds are at Wood Buffalo National Park in central Canada. From here, each autumn, the cranes travel huge distances across the middle of North America to the Aransas National Wildlife Refuge in Texas, covering as much as 800 km in a day. Thanks to careful conservation measures and habitat management, the population wintering at Aransas is now well over 200, with an estimated world population of 336 birds.

In addition, a small group of cranes has been introduced near Lake Kissimmee in central Florida, and they have successfully bred there, while in 2006 a pair bred in Wisconsin for the first time in over a century. The Wisconsin parent birds had been hatched in captivity at a research centre in Maryland, and had then flown behind a light aircraft from Wisconsin to Florida. Amazingly, they were then able to use their innate migratory ability to return to Wisconsin!

Today, visitors to either Wood Buffalo or central Florida can sometimes witness the extraordinary courtship dance of the Whooping Crane – complete with the loud, whooping call, usually uttered during a duet between male and female, that gives the species its name.

As a large, low-flying migrant, however, it faces many hazards, including collisions with power lines, wind farms and other structures. A major oil spill off the Texas coast could also pollute their refuge at Aransas. But, with continued effort, and a modicum of luck, the Whooping Crane should continue to survive and thrive.

Tall, rare and beautiful – the Whooping Crane

Grus americana | # WHOOPING CRANE

DESPITE ALL THE CONSERVATION EFFORTS DEVOTED TO THIS MAGNIFICENT, ICONIC BIRD, THE WHOOPING CRANE IS STILL NOT COMPLETELY SAFE

Like so many of the world's 15 species of crane, the Red-crowned (also known as the Japanese) Crane combines beauty and rarity in equal measure. Second only to the Whooping Crane in the rarity stakes, the current world population is estimated at between 1,700 and 2,000 birds.

The breeding range of the Red-crowned Crane is highly fragmented, with a population breeding in northeast China and the extreme southeast of Russia, which winters in Korea and China, and a resident population on the island of Hokkaido in northern Japan.

It is the Japanese group which has captured the imagination of observers for centuries, due to the extraordinary courtship dance performed by breeding pairs. Long celebrated in art and literature, this elaborate and beautiful ritual, which evolved to strengthen the monogamous pair bond, has inspired generations of human dancers to imitate the cranes. During the dance, the birds' red crown fills with blood, making it swell and become more brightly coloured. This may be used to communicate excitement or to respond to aggression from a rival bird.

Not surprisingly for such a striking bird, the Red-crowned Crane has a large body of folklore associated with it. In Japan it was believed that the crane achieved extraordinary longevity, living over a thousand years. In China, the species features frequently in fairy tales, and its Chinese name, *xian he*, translates as 'Celestial Crane'. In Chinese art, cranes are often used to depict the souls of recently departed people on their journey to heaven.

But the most moving story associated with the Red-crowned Crane is that of a young girl, Sadako Sasaki. Just two when the atom bomb was dropped on Hiroshima, Sadako survived but, ten years later, she was diagnosed with leukaemia caused by the radiation. Inspired by an ancient Japanese belief that if a person folds one thousand paper cranes the gods grant them a wish, Sadako began work — but sadly died before she could complete her task. Following her death, children from all over Japan, and later across the world, began to fold paper cranes as a symbol of peace, a tradition that continues to this day.

Today, the Japanese population of Red-crowned Cranes is doing well, not least because the cranes are a major tourist attraction, bringing valuable revenue to the island of Hokkaido. However, the future of the 1,400 or so birds breeding in China is far less secure. The Chinese government is said to view the area where the cranes breed as its 'great northern food basket', and draining of wetlands is happening on a massive scale. The Three Gorges Dam, being built along the Yangtze River, where many Chinese cranes spend the winter, is a major threat to the species' future.

The dancing display of the Red-crowned Crane, in Hokkaido, Japan

Grus japonensis | # RED-CROWNED CRANE

THROUGHOUT ITS RANGE THE RED-CROWNED CRANE IS REVERED AS A SYMBOL OF GOOD LUCK AND FIDELITY IN MARRIAGE, AND APPEARS ON JAPANESE BRIDAL KIMONOS

One of the few birds whose English and scientific names are both an onomatopoeic representation of its call, the Corncrake is justly famous as a creature which, although often heard, is very rarely seen. The 19th-century poet John Clare described the bird as 'but a summer noise among the meadow hay', which perfectly epitomises its mysterious, elusive nature.

Visitors to the Corncrake's breeding grounds in the Western Isles of Scotland, or the marshes of eastern Europe, often complain of being kept awake at night by its astonishingly loud, repetitive call. But unless they are remarkably persistent – or just plain lucky – they hardly ever catch more than a glimpse of this elusive little bird.

The Corncrake is a member of the rail family – though, unlike the majority of its relatives, it shuns the aquatic lifestyle. Instead, as its name suggests, it is a farmland bird. More specifically, it is suited to traditional agriculture, with damp meadows, long grass and a sympathetic mowing regime – reducing the danger of the chicks being killed at harvest time.

Because such timeless farming methods have almost disappeared – in northwest Europe at least – the Corncrake has suffered a serious decline in recent years. In Britain, since Clare's day, the Corncrake has gone from being one of our most widespread birds to being found only on a few Scottish islands where the traditional crofting lifestyle is still practised. However, after almost a century's absence, Corn-crakes are now being reintroduced to England, in the marshes of East Anglia.

The species also suffers from problems of habitat loss during migration, though, for the time being at least, its African wintering grounds appear to be safe. Watching a Corncrake fluttering across a hay meadow, in the odd moments when it breaks cover at all, it seems incredible that such an ungainly flyer is able to travel more than 8,000 km from its European and west Asian breeding grounds to the savannahs of Tanzania, Mozambique and South Africa – yet it completes this return journey every year, travelling mainly under the cover of darkness.

In common with most long-distance migrants, the Corncrake occasionally goes off course: vagrants have turned up over a surprisingly wide geographical area from Greenland to Bermuda and the Seychelles to Australia. One theory suggests that the Corncrake's reluctance to take to the air may be matched by an equal reluctance to stop once airborne! Ultimately this wanderlust may prove to be the species' salvation, enabling it to take advantage of new habitats if its old ones prove unsuitable.

A lucky glimpse of the elusive Corncrake

CORNCRAKE | *Crex crex*

THE BEST WAY TO SEE A CORNCRAKE IS TO MIMIC THE RHYTHM OF ITS CALL; TRY A
CREDIT CARD SCRAPED ACROSS THE TEETH OF A METAL COMB

The rail family has the unenviable distinction of having had more species become extinct in historical times (since 1600) than any other family of birds. Were it not for an extraordinary discovery in a remote part of New Zealand's South Island in 1948, the current count of extinct rails would stand at 12 rather than 11.

It was in 1948 that ornithologists exploring the Fiordland region near the very southwest tip of the South Island stumbled across the Takahe. This remarkable flightless bird had been considered extinct for 50 years – with only four previous sightings at all. Since its rediscovery, the Takahe's hold on existence has continued to be tenuous. However, thanks to careful conservation measures, the world population now stands at an estimated 150 birds. Another 60 or so individuals have been introduced to various offshore islands to maintain a safety-net in case disaster should befall the original population.

Like many of its smaller relatives, the dozen or so species of gallinules, the Takahe's plumage is a combination of purple, blue and green, with purple predominant. The Takahe has huge red legs and an enormous pinkish-red bill, which it uses to pluck its favoured food: the bases of grassy tussocks, which require plenty of effort to dig up. In winter, when snows arrive and cover their food supply, the birds descend into the surrounding valleys, where they feed on the rhizomes of ferns until the snow melts and they can return to their summer home.

Like other flightless species, the Takahe has wings that are purely vestigial, though they are still used during courtship displays. Flightlessness evolved in the Takahe, as in so many island-dwelling species, because there were no land predators in New Zealand – at least until white settlers arrived in the eighteenth century bringing with them a host of animals including dogs, cats and rats; following which the fate of many flightless birds was a rapid extinction. This is what happened to the Takahes of the North Island, which may indeed have been a separate species from the South Island ones.

In recent times, the main threat to the continued survival of the species has come from deer, which overgraze the habitat, leading to food shortages and ultimately lowering the Takahe's breeding success. The control and removal of the deer – often using helicopters in order to gain access to this remote region – has improved matters. Even so, the Takahe population of Fiordland remains very vulnerable. To counter this, since the early 1980s conservationists have run a captive-breeding programme, which should safeguard the future of the species.

The endangered Takahe in its native New Zealand

TAKAHE | *Porphyrio hochstetteri*

THE TAKAHE HAS TO BE SEEN TO BE BELIEVED. THE WORLD'S LARGEST LIVING RAIL, IT STANDS HALF A METRE HIGH AND CAN WEIGH UP TO 3 KG, WITH MALES SIGNIFICANTLY HEAVIER THAN FEMALES

When it comes to the classification of the world's birds, there are some species that simply do not fit into any established pattern. The Kagu, an extraordinary ghost-like bird found on a single archipelago in the Pacific Ocean, is one of them.

Though originally considered to be related to the herons and egrets, the Kagu has long baffled taxonomists. It has several unique features, including a special membrane covering its nostrils, and it has a blood composition unlike any other bird, with a much lower red-blood-cell count, yet with higher haemoglobin.

The Kagu is entirely confined to the French territory of New Caledonia, in the northwestern Pacific, where it lives in native forests from sea level to an altitude of about 1,400 m. It is a medium-sized, flightless bird, about the size and shape of a Cattle Egret. However, being flightless, the Kagu is more than twice as heavy.

The bird's most obvious feature is that unlike almost all other ground-dwelling forest birds, which tend to have cryptic coloration for camouflage purposes, its plumage is very pale: a delicate ash-grey, shading into a dirty white on the crown and belly. It also has very large, well-developed wings, rather than the vestigial ones usually possessed by flightless birds, though because these lack

The Kagu has well-developed wings, despite being a flightless bird

flight muscles it is unable to get airborne. It does use its wings, which are patterned with alternating dark and light stripes, during courtship displays, which may explain why they have remained relatively long.

Another striking feature of the Kagu is its large eyes, with excellent binocular vision – again, this is unusual in that the bird is primarily diurnal. These may have evolved to enable the Kagu to feed in dense forest, as they are clearly an advantage when foraging for food. During feeding the advantage of those nasal coverings becomes apparent: they prevent dirt from entering the bird's nostrils as it grubs around.

The species has always been at the centre of local customs, with the feathers used in ornamental head-dresses, and the bird – known locally as 'Ghost of the Forest' – being hunted and eaten. Until the arrival of white settlers this was not a major problem, but since Captain Cook's *Endeavour* landed on New Caledonia in the 1770s, bringing the usual cargo of dogs, cats and pigs, the Kagu has been constantly under threat. A large feral population of dogs on the islands remains a major problem.

The Kagu's low reproductive rate – a maximum of a single chick each year – has not helped it maintain its population: fewer than 1,000 birds now remain in the wild. The future of the Kagu contains one ray of hope, however: its striking appearance and links with local culture have made it into a tourist attraction and emblem of New Caledonia.

KAGU | *Rhynochetos jubatus*

THE KAGU HAS AN EXTRAORDINARY VOICE, WITH A RANGE OF CALLS INCLUDING A DAWN DUET BETWEEN THE MALE AND FEMALE THAT HAS BEEN DESCRIBED AS SOUNDING LIKE A CROSS BETWEEN A CROWING ROOSTER AND A PUPPY!

One of the most unusual and sought-after species of Central and South America, the Sunbittern is another taxonomic puzzle. Indeed, it is so distinctive that it merits its own family — one of just 23 so-called 'monotypic' families in the world.

With its distinctive horizontal posture, the Sunbittern superficially resembles a rather oddly-shaped heron. It also shares its cryptic plumage with several species of bittern (hence its English name), so one could be forgiven for assuming that its closest relatives are members of the heron family. Other scientists have noticed similarities with the painted-snipes of Africa and South America.

However, like the similarly problematic Kagu, it has ultimately been granted a place in that varied group of birds known as the Gruiformes, an order which includes cranes, rails and bustards. Latest scientific research suggests that despite their very obvious differences in appearance and lifestyle, the Sunbittern and the Kagu may share a common ancestor, and that the two species diversified when the ancient landmass of Gondwanaland broke up, starting some 200 million years ago.

Today, the Sunbittern's range extends from Guatemala and Costa Rica, down through the Orinoco and Amazon basins, to central Brazil — though its secretive habits mean that it is very hard to estimate true numbers and distribution. It lives in humid rainforests, always near fresh water, as it feeds almost entirely on aquatic organisms — everything from dragonflies and shrimps to frogs and eels.

The Sunbittern's striking plumage is one of its most attractive features: a subtle mixture of browns, blacks and greys forming vermiculated patterns. But its most prominent feature is only revealed when the bird opens its wings: striking chestnut patches on the upper wings and tail, which are fanned out in an incredible display. Once thought to be for courtship, it is now believed that these amazing patterns are used mainly for defensive purposes, to ward off potential predators such as kites and ocelots.

Sunbitterns are attentive parents, with both the male and the female feeding the two or three chicks, and guarding them against intruders by using their threat display. The young Sunbittern is unusual in that it does not have a juvenile plumage, passing directly from downy chick to adult in a single moult. Even youngsters are able to perform the 'frontal display', which may explain the early adoption of full adult plumage.

Oddly for such an elusive bird, Sunbitterns adapt well to captivity, and have been kept by native peoples in Brazil and Venezuela, as well as by various institutions. A pair was kept at London Zoo as early as the 1860s, where they bred successfully.

The Sunbittern's striking plumage during a threat display

Eurypyga helias | # SUNBITTERN

LIKE HERONS, SUNBITTERNS USE STEALTH TO STALK THEIR PREY, CREEPING UP ON THEIR INTENDED TARGET BEFORE STRIKING FORWARD, USING POWERFUL NECK MUSCLES TO SEIZE IT WITH THAT FEARSOME BILL

The Great Bustard of Europe and central Asia shares with its African relative, the Kori Bustard, the title of the heaviest living creature able to fly. With males weighing as much as 18 kg, they comfortably beat potential competitors such as Old World vultures (maximum weight 12.5 kg), condors (15 kg) and swans (15 kg).

Early in the spring, the male bustard seeks out an elevated site, inflates his gular sac (a pouch at the front of his neck), lifts his tail to reveal the bright white undertail-coverts, and fans his wings. Even more incredibly, he then appears virtually to turn himself inside out, creating a bizarre morph of his original shape. The whole performance is to attract a mate, and is visible from some distance away.

What is unique about the Great Bustard's display is that, unlike other bustards, the male does not actually hold a territory, but instead uses the lekking system favoured by a diverse range of other bird species including Black Grouse and Great Snipe. Unlike other lekking species, however, the males rarely fight each other. Instead, each keeps his distance from his potential rivals, relying purely on the visual display to entice a female to breed.

Outside the breeding season the Great Bustard is a very sociable bird, forming flocks of up to 50 birds. The European populations generally remain on or near their breeding area all year round, dispersing short distances during harsh weather, but the Asian birds do migrate south to avoid the worst excesses of the winter. Birds from the population recently reintroduced onto Salisbury Plain in southern England have also wandered in winter, some as far afield as France.

Great Bustards have suffered major population declines in the past century or so, largely because their need for large, undisturbed areas of insect-rich grassland has come into conflict with modern farming techniques, which have rendered large areas of habitat unsuitable for breeding. Hunting has also been a problem in the past, and continues to be an issue in Ukraine and China, while disturbance can also reduce breeding success.

As a result of all these problems, the Great Bustard became extinct in many western European countries during the 19th century, and in more recent times it has suffered population declines in eastern Europe. Areas where they continue to thrive are the plains of central Spain and parts of European Russia, which between them support about 25,000 birds out of a total world population estimated at about 35,000.

*The heaviest living creature that
can fly – the Great Bustard*

GREAT BUSTARD | *Otis tarda*

WATCHING A FLOCK OF GREAT BUSTARDS TAKE TO THE AIR OVER THE PLAINS OF
CENTRAL SPAIN OR EASTERN EUROPE IS A TRULY AWESOME EXPERIENCE, MATCHED
ONLY BY THEIR EXTRAORDINARY COURTSHIP DISPLAY

Few birds evoke such fascination as the Ibisbill, an enigmatic and distinctive wader found in the mountainous regions of Central Asia. Unlike many other highland river dwellers, however, the Ibisbill does not seek out fast-flowing bubbling streams where the water dashes across the rocks. Instead, it prefers to feed in the slower, flatter parts of rivers, enabling it to use that extraordinary bill to its full effect: wading into deep water to probe between the boulders lying on the riverbed. Another feeding method is to stand still – sometimes for several hours on end – and simply pick up small insects and other invertebrates such as caddisfly larvae as they drift past on the water's surface.

Taxonomically lying somewhere between the oystercatchers and the stilts and avocets, the Ibisbill has long merited its own single-species family. Despite its rather specialised habitat requirements, it has a large range, stretching from Kazakhstan and Kashmir in the west, through Tibet and the extreme north of India, to eastern China.

Like many birds of this high-altitude region, it moves down to lower altitudes in autumn to avoid frozen conditions – sometimes descending several thousand metres to spend the winter as low as 100 m above sea level. It remains mainly solitary all year round, apart of course from when breeding, though flocks and roosts of up to 25 birds have occasionally been recorded. Unless disturbed they rarely take to the wing; instead they often perform a rather peculiar display in which the bird moves its head rapidly up and down in what appears to be a nervous twitch.

Because of its remote haunts, the breeding behaviour of the Ibisbill has not been closely studied. We do know that it generally chooses to nest on shingle areas beside rivers, where the browns, blacks, greys and whites of its plumage make it surprisingly inconspicuous, especially when it tucks that distinctive bill under its wing. Because the breeding season presents only a brief window of opportunity at these altitudes, Ibisbills often begin laying well before the end of the snow season, meaning that if winter is prolonged the incubating bird may become entirely covered with a layer of snow.

As far as can be ascertained, the Ibisbill is not yet globally threatened – partly because its haunts are so far from centres of human activity, and partly because it has such an extensive, albeit somewhat fragmented, range. Indeed perhaps the greatest threat to the Ibisbill is the opening up of its breeding areas to tourism and recreational activities, which could lead to disturbance.

The Ibisbill's curiously decurved bill and striking plumage

IBISBILL | *Ibidorhyncha struthersii*

THE IBISBILL'S COMBINATION OF STUNNING PLUMAGE AND CURIOUSLY DECURVED BILL, AND ITS PREFERENCE FOR FEEDING ON HIGH-ELEVATION MOUNTAIN RIVERS, MAKE IT HIGHLY SOUGHT-AFTER BY BIRDERS

The Black-winged Stilt of Europe, Asia and Africa, together with its three close relatives in Australasia and the Americas – now considered to be distinctive species in their own right – are typical birds of marshy areas in all the equatorial, tropical and warm-temperate areas of the world. Even to the non-birder they stand out – quite literally – by virtue of their enormously long legs, the longest relative to their overall body-length of all the world's birds.

Typically, therefore, they are found in a wide range of freshwater, brackish and saltwater wetlands: from temporary ponds and flooded fields to swamps, marshes and lakes. Highly adaptable, they can survive at high altitudes as well as close to sea level: the White-backed (or Southern) Stilt reaches heights of 4,200 m in the Puna Zone between the Andes and the Amazon in South America. Stilts are also able to thrive in salt pans and alkaline lakes, often seen in the company of huge flocks of flamingos, another famously long-legged wading bird.

One reason for stilts' adaptability is their catholic choice of diet: they feed on a wide range of small aquatic insects and their larvae, but have also been known to take seeds, tadpoles, fish eggs and crustaceans, depending on what is available from place to place and season to season. They usually feed by wading through deep water and picking items off the surface.

Being such a wide-ranging group of birds, the timing of their breeding is also very variable. Like most tropical and equatorial birds, stilts in these areas usually vary their start of nesting depending on the timing of the seasonal rains. In the more temperate parts of their range, stilts follow the normal pattern of breeding during the northern or southern spring and summer.

Incubating the eggs presents something of a challenge: to do so the male or female stilt needs to tuck its legs up behind it in what appears to be a very uncomfortable position. Despite appearances, however, the birds appear perfectly content. Baby stilts are miniature versions of their parents, complete with amazingly long legs – though in the first day or two after hatching they do look quite precarious as they wobble about.

Though the original species has been split into no fewer than four separate ones (Black-winged, Black-necked, White-backed and White-headed Stilts), fortunately all four populations have healthy numbers; though the Hawaiian race – now considered a subspecies of the Black-necked Stilt of the Americas – is considered vulnerable, as its limited range supports just 1,800 birds.

An pair of Black-winged Stilts displaying

Himantopus himantopus | # BLACK-WINGED STILT

THE COURTSHIP DISPLAY IS, AS ONE MIGHT EXPECT FROM SUCH AN ELEGANT BIRD, HIGHLY THEATRICAL: THE BIRDS PERFORM ALL SORTS OF ACROBATIC LEAPS AND FLIGHTS IN ORDER TO IMPRESS EACH OTHER AND STRENGTHEN THE PAIR BOND

How does a crocodile clean its teeth? According to received wisdom, by allowing a small wading bird to enter its mouth, where it picks off pieces of stuck and rotting food. Surely this is the perfect example of a symbiotic relationship: the crocodile gets his teeth cleaned, while the bird gets a free meal.

The story of the 'crocodile bird' – or to give its correct name, Egyptian Plover – goes back more than two millennia, to the year 459 BC. In that year, the Greek historian Herodotus – known to later generations as 'the father of history' – paid a visit to Egypt, and wrote that he had witnessed a small bird picking food from the jaws of a Nile Crocodile.

Many years later, this was apparently confirmed by various observers, including the 19th-century German ornithologist Alfred Brehm, and the British ornithologist Richard Meinertzhagen in the early 20th century. The latter's reputation for exaggeration (and at times complete fabrication) should have rung alarm bells, and indeed there is no evidence at all that the stories of the 'Crocodile Bird' are true.

Disappointing though this may be, the Egyptian Plover is nevertheless a remarkable bird. Handsome and attractive, the plumage is a striking combination of pale ochre beneath and blue-grey above, with a black breast-band extending over the back, and a black head and neck with a prominent white eye-stripe. These features, together with the bird's legendary approachability, make it a favourite with birders, especially bird photographers.

The range of the Egyptian Plover extends in a broad band across the centre of sub-Saharan Africa, mainly north of the equator. Its preferred habitat is large tropical rivers in lowland areas, with plenty of sand and gravel, where the birds both feed and nest. They generally breed early in the year, when water levels are at their lowest, to avoid the risk of flooding. The eggs are laid in a shallow scrape, and when the bird leaves the nest to feed they are covered with sand to reduce the risk of being taken by predators.

But it is after the chicks hatch that the Egyptian Plover's breeding behaviour really becomes interesting. Uniquely amongst birds, the parents regularly cover their chicks with sand until they are three or four weeks old, not just as a defence against predators but also to reduce the effects of the hot sun. The male and female also soak their lower belly feathers in water, using this to cool down their young, either by applying it directly or by allowing the chicks to drink.

Crocodile Bird or Egyptian Plover
– either way, this bird is a
favourite with birders

EGYPTIAN PLOVER | *Pluvianus aegyptius*

ONCE PLACED IN A SEPARATE FAMILY, FOR SOME TIME NOW THE EGYPTIAN PLOVER HAS BEEN CLASSIFIED WITH THE COURSERS AND PRATINCOLES, A DIVERSE FAMILY OF WADERS FOUND MAINLY IN THE TROPICAL REGIONS OF AFRICA AND ASIA

Of all the wading birds of Europe, surely none is held in such affection as the Northern Lapwing. One reason for its popularity is the bird's sheer beauty: the subtle shades of its plumage and the prominent crest. Another is its sound: the insistent, high-pitched call that gives the species one of its many alternative names, Peewit. But perhaps the main reason is that we have lived alongside Lapwings, and farmed the land they depend on, giving us an ancient bond going back to the earliest days of civilisation.

For, in Britain at least, the Lapwing is mainly a bird of agricultural areas: breeding in wet meadows alongside horses and cattle, and wintering in huge flocks on stubble fields. That has been the Lapwing's downfall: the type of farming it depends on has rapidly disappeared across great swathes of its range, forcing it to depend mainly on the specially managed habitat of bird reserves. As a result, the Lapwing's population has declined dramatically, although it remains one of Europe's most widespread breeding birds, with large populations also found on the steppes of central Asia as far east as China.

At the start of the breeding season, the male Lapwing performs an acrobatic song-flight designed both to ward off potential rivals and to impress his mate. This consists of as many as eight

The Lapwing is one of the most recognisable of birds with its attractive plumage and crest

different 'tricks', including flying rapidly up into the air, rolling from side to side, and plummeting down towards the earth. As well as showing off his flying skills, he calls as he does so, creating an impressive courtship spectacle.

Once the eggs are laid in a shallow scrape in the ground – and especially after the chicks have hatched – both male and female Lapwings are constantly on the alert for possible intruders, which might steal their eggs or harm their offspring.

Once the breeding season is finished, Lapwings gather in large flocks – sometimes numbering several thousand birds – and spend the winter on farmland, often in the company of Golden Plovers. Lapwings, however, are especially susceptible to cold weather, and will often move some distance to avoid it. As a result, the species has occasionally crossed the Atlantic, as they did during the winter of 1927/28, when hundreds of Lapwings caught up in a cold-weather movement appeared in Newfoundland.

Curiously, the name of the species does not refer, as might be assumed, to the bird's style of flight. It apparently derives from an Old English term meaning 'movable crest', which, as the original meaning became obscure, was corrupted first into 'lapwinch', then 'lappinch', and finally 'lapwing'.

NORTHERN LAPWING | *Vanellus vanellus*

THE LAPWING'S ABILITY TO SPOT PREDATORS AND SEE THEM OFF ENCOURAGES
WADERS OF OTHER SPECIES TO NEST ALONGSIDE THEM, WHERE THEY
ARE MORE LIKELY TO BE SAFE

Despite a population numbering in the millions, and a global range extending across six of the world's seven continents, the Red Knot has been described as potentially the first casualty of global climate change. This is because the species has, more than almost any other, evolved a lifestyle which is utterly dependent on the timing of the seasons.

As the austral summer comes towards its end – about the same time as the spring equinox in Europe, Asia and North America – vast flocks of Red Knot scattered across the southern hemisphere begin to grow restless. They are responding to minute changes in day-length that over centuries of evolutionary adaptation have identified the optimum time to set off on their northward migration.

This is a journey that will take them all the way from the coasts of southern South America, South Africa and Australasia, via North America, Europe and Asia, to their breeding grounds high in the Arctic. Here, like so many long-distance migrants that travel between the northern and southern hemispheres, they take advantage of the astonishing bonanza of insect food characteristic of the brief Arctic summer.

Normally weighing about 100 g, Knots feed frantically in the days before they set off, putting on fat in a subcutaneous layer beneath their feathers and skin. In doing so, they more than double their weight, to as much as 220 g. Following this binge they will fly almost 15,000 km in a few huge leaps, rather than the short hops favoured by many other migrating birds.

Because they have so few stopover points, those they do favour assume a higher importance than for other species. So the commercial fishing of horseshoe crabs in the Delaware Bay area, on the east coast of the United States, has had serious implications for the tens of thousands of Knots that rely on the crabs' eggs as they refuel on their journey north.

Once Knot arrive in the Arctic, in late May, they get down to breeding at once. This is where the problems increase. Red Knot have very specialised breeding requirements: the tundra on which they nest has characteristically short vegetation, which is now altering dramatically due to the effects of higher temperatures caused by global warming. The longer growing season allows insects to peak earlier, meaning that by the time the Knot chicks hatch there may not be enough food for them to eat. Unlike species breeding further south, the Red Knot cannot shift its range northwards in response to the changes – quite simply, it has nowhere left to go.

The name that puzzles so many people is, like so many bird names, a representation of its grunting call. Until the 18th century, the 'k' would have been pronounced, giving a more accurate rendering of the call.

A huge flock of Red Knot takes to the air in Norfolk, England

Calidris canutus | # RED KNOT

THE ABILITY OF THE RED KNOT TO MAKE ITS INCREDIBLE JOURNEY IS TRULY ONE OF THE MIRACLES OF THE BIRD WORLD

Most species of wader, especially those in the large, sprawling family containing sandpipers, snipes, curlews, godwits and their allies, have a fairly cryptic plumage, often with subtle markings enabling them to blend in to the background vegetation if necessary. Not so the male Ruff.

Outside the breeding season the Ruff is not a particularly conspicuous bird. But, as spring approaches, he adopts an extraordinary outfit: comprising not only the ruff around the neck that gives the species its name, but also head tufts and wattles. These are used in the famous communal lek – an annual tournament in which rival males joust with each other much in the manner of medieval knights, in order to gain advantage when it comes to breeding.

This bizarre plumage only applies to the male Ruff. Females (known as reeves) and juveniles sport a typical combination of plainish brown or grey underparts and scalloped upperparts. Females are also appreciably smaller and lighter than the males.

The male's head-dresses come in a wide variety of colours, ranging from almost pure black, to a rich chestnut, to snow white – with a whole gamut of intermediate colours and patterns. They give the bird a bizarre, front-heavy appearance, made almost comical by the contrast with the Ruff's bare face, small eye and rather pathetic, drooping bill.

But once the action begins, the Ruff changes from a comical creature into a lean, mean fighting machine – amply justifying its scientific name *Philomachus pugnax*, a combination of Greek and Latin meaning 'fighter who loves fighting'!

The Ruff's lek is arguably the most complex and fascinating form of courtship behaviour found in any species of bird. Each 'resident' male defends a small part of the lek against other males, using his powerful feet and bill to jab at his rival. They adopt a variety of stylised postures, such as thrusting the bill forwards, vibrating the tail and lifting the wings. When the females arrive, the males become even more frenzied in their movements, fluttering their wings as if welcoming their potential mates.

What makes the Ruff's lek unique amongst birds is the presence of outsiders known as 'satellite males'. These individuals, often sporting white ruffs, hang around on the edge of the arena, and instead of fighting they wait. As the females arrive, they try to sneak a mating, and often succeed, thus proving that brains are sometimes better than brawn.

As with other lekking birds, after mating the males play no further part in the incubation of eggs or raising of young, leaving all the work to the females. Lekking is extremely rare in birds, and can only exist where there is an ample supply of food, thus removing the need for a male to defend a permanent territory.

The male Ruff's head-dress is used to great effect during the lek

Philomachus pugnax | RUFF

THE MALE RUFF'S EXTRAORDINARY VARIETY OF HEAD-DRESSES COMBINES WITH OUTRAGEOUS SOCIAL BEHAVIOUR TO CREATE WHAT MUST SURELY BE THE MOST EXTROVERT OF THE WADERS

Hong Kong may not seem the likeliest place to see one of the world's rarest birds. But the Mai Po Marshes have a deserved reputation as a hotspot for migrating waders. And amongst the vast flocks of Red-necked Stints, a careful observer may be able to pick out the much rarer Spoon-billed Sandpiper.

Apart from its rarity, the Spoon-billed Sandpiper is on every birder's 'must-see' list because of the extraordinary adaptation that gives it its name: its flattened spatulate bill, unique amongst waders.

Rather like a miniature Spoonbill, this species feeds by sweeping its bill from side to side. Yet like other small sandpipers and stints it feeds mainly on tiny aquatic invertebrates, together with terrestrial insects, seeds and other morsels picked off the water's surface. Occasionally it has, like other waders, been observed using a 'foot-paddling' technique. This entails the bird rapidly moving its foot in the water, stirring up the mud and stimulating tiny creatures to come to the surface, where they can be easily picked off.

The flat, spatulate bill of a Spoon-billed Sandpiper, on its breeding grounds in Siberia

The species breeds in the extreme northeast corner of Asia, from the Chukotskiy (or Chukchi) Peninsula south to Kamchatka – one of the most inaccessible places in the world, and almost impossible to survey. Even in this vast area they never nest further than six km from the sea, choosing areas with sandy ridges covered with sparse coastal vegetation, usually amongst salt marshes. Studies have shown that they are monogamous and highly site-faithful, with two out of three birds returning to the same breeding area each spring.

After leaving their breeding grounds in early autumn, Spoon-billed Sandpipers take a coastal route southwards, stopping off at various places including Japan, North Korea and South Korea. They winter across a wide area, from south China to southern India and Sri Lanka, but nowhere are they common.

Indeed, Spoon-billed Sandpiper is now one of the rarest of the 80 or so species in its family, though limited knowledge about its breeding and wintering ranges makes finding accurate population figures difficult. Nevertheless, estimates of just 400 to 1,000 breeding pairs (probably nearer the lower figure) give some idea of its extremely parlous situation.

Given that that very little can affect them in their remote breeding areas, it is thought that the decline in numbers is due to loss of habitat at migrating stopover points such as Saemangeum in South Korea, which is being drained and used for industry.

Eurynorhynchus pygmeus

SPOON-BILLED SANDPIPER

Waders appear to be particularly prone to unusual sexual behaviour, and the Red-necked Phalarope is a case in point. Like the Grey (Red) and Wilson's Phalaropes, it displays reverse sexual dimorphism. To put it simply, the female is the dominant partner, controlling courtship and allowing the male to do all the work. This means that the male incubates the eggs and raises the chicks entirely on his own, but also that the female takes the lead in courting, defending a territory and mating, with females often squabbling for advantage as the males look on. It also means that the bird with the duller, more cryptic plumage is the male; the female Red-necked Phalarope sports a much smarter outfit, with cleaner lines, darker plumage and a brighter, more extensive rufous patch on the neck.

Phalaropes are unusual amongst wading birds in that they habitually swim. The local Shetland dialect name for the species is *pirrie duc*, meaning 'little duck', and that is exactly what these diminutive birds – barely larger than a sparrow – resemble as they potter about at the edge of shallow, marshy lakes in search of tiny insects to eat.

Both their scientific and English names derive from the Greek words for 'coot-footed', referring to the tiny webbed lobes of skin that make propulsion through the water possible in the manner of that species. Indeed, the bird was once known as 'Red Coot-footed *Tringa*', though the name phalarope gained the upper hand when introduced by ornithologist Thomas Pennant in 1776.

The Red-necked Phalarope has a largely circumpolar breeding distribution, from Alaska and Canada through Greenland, Iceland, northern Scandinavia, and across Siberia. Though mostly found around the Arctic Circle, they nest in small numbers as far south as the Outer Hebrides in Britain, and the Aleutian Islands in the Bering Sea between Russia and Alaska – which are on the same latitude as London.

After breeding, Red-necked Phalaropes head out to sea, where they appear to relish bobbing about like corks on giant waves. Wintering populations are known from such diverse locations as the Humboldt Current off Peru and the Arabian Sea.

On migration they will often gather in huge flocks, with two million or more at the Bay of Fundy, on Canada's Atlantic coast, and tens of thousands seen at Mono Lake in California and Great Salt Lake in Utah. Where some of these birds actually spend the winter is still a mystery, proving that even with a species as common as this, we still have much to learn.

The Red-necked Phalarope is a wader, but is also able to swim

RED-NECKED PHALAROPE | *Phalaropus lobatus*

The classification and naming of birds has always been a difficult business, and at no time more so than during the 19th century, when so many of the world's birds were discovered. So we can sympathise with the great ornithologist John Gould, who on being presented with two specimens caught near Adelaide – one noticeably brighter and more colourful than the other – identified them as two separate species.

Once his error had been discovered, the two specimens were given the name Plains-wanderer. But there was another surprise in store. Closer examination revealed that the brighter and more colourful bird was in fact the female.

This phenomenon, known to scientists as 'reverse sexual dimorphism', is extremely rare in birds – the Eurasian Dotterel and all three species of phalarope are exceptions. These species, like the Plains-wanderer, also practise a breeding strategy known as 'serial polyandry', in which a single female mates with more than one male during a single breeding season. Once they have mated, and she has laid her clutch of eggs, she takes no further part in the duties of incubating the eggs and raising the young.

The Plains-wanderer was placed in the order Gruiformes at first, because of its obvious resemblance in appearance and habits to the

The female Plains-wanderer is the more colourful of the pair, sporting a distinctive 'necklace'

button-quails, but more recently the species has been shifted into the world's second-largest order of birds, the *Charadriiformes*. This is based on detailed study of the bird's anatomy; its habits, including its characteristic wader-like run; and in particular its eggs, which have the pointed ends typical of members of this order.

Like many birds of open grasslands, the Plains-wanderer is highly terrestrial, preferring to walk or run rather than fly when threatened by a predator or intruder. It uses its long legs to stand on tiptoe to survey its surroundings; if threatened it may also crouch flat on the ground, using its cryptic camouflage to avoid being seen. Its evasion techniques are so successful that for many years it was assumed to be nocturnal, though in fact it is mainly active at dawn and dusk.

The Plains-wanderer has the misfortune to live in a region where land is in great demand: the open grasslands of eastern Australia. Since European settlers first arrived here in the late 18th century, much of its former habitat has been converted into pasture for livestock or fields for arable crops – neither of which suit this species. As a result its habitat has become highly fragmented, and numbers have plummeted: down to between 2,500 and 8,000 birds – meriting 'Endangered' status. Urgent action will be needed if this unique species is not to enter a terminal decline.

PLAINS-WANDERER | *Pedionomus torquatus*

SINCE ITS INITIAL DISCOVERY, THE PLAINS-WANDERER HAS REMAINED SOMETHING OF A MYSTERY. LIKE OTHER SINGLE-SPECIES FAMILIES, IT HAS CAUSED THE TAXONOMISTS MANY HEADACHES

Why any bird would choose to spend the winter months within the Arctic Circle is beyond imagining, but one kind of gull does just that. After having finished breeding, Ross's Gull heads north from its Siberian and Canadian nesting areas, to overwinter on the edge of the Arctic Ocean's pack-ice.

Ross's Gull is named after the great 19th-century explorer James Clark Ross, who spent much of his life searching for the fabled Northwest Passage connecting the Atlantic Ocean to China, discovered the Magnetic North Pole, and even led an expedition to Antarctica. The bird itself was discovered as late as July 1823, when the young James Ross managed to shoot one on an expedition to northern Canada, and it was named after him the following year. Ross himself was in no doubt that he had collected a very special bird, drawing attention to 'the beautiful tint of a most delicate rose colour on its breast' – indicating that the bird was an adult in breeding plumage.

Another sixty years passed before the first nest of Ross's Gull was discovered, in western Greenland in 1885. Twenty years later, in 1905, the Russian explorer Sergei Buturlin stumbled across the main breeding area of the species. This was not, as Ross himself had surmised, high in the Arctic pack-ice, but in the relatively benign region of eastern Siberia, at a marshy area of the Kolyma Delta.

Ross's Gull is also the subject of a curious controversy: the very first British record, from the inland town of Tadcaster in February 1847, is one of several very dubious specimens processed by the same taxidermist which have earned the nickname the 'Tadcaster Rarities'. This record has now been expunged from the official British List.

As late as the eve of World War II, British ornithologist Bernard Tucker could write that 'very few ornithologists [or indeed anyone else] have seen this gull alive', while his contemporary James Fisher described it as 'one of the most mysterious birds in the world'. Partly this is due to its extreme rarity: despite a recent increase, there are still fewer than 100 records for Britain, while in the lower 48 states of the USA it is also very rare.

Another reason for the popularity of Ross's Gull amongst birders on both sides of the Atlantic is its great beauty – not a word one usually associates with gulls. But a Ross's Gull in full breeding plumage, its dove-grey upperparts contrasting with pale, rosy-tinged underparts and a neat black collar, is a sight to convert even the most ardent gull-hater.

The beautiful and almost mythical
Ross's Gull

ROSS'S GULL | *Rhodostethia rosea*

AMONGST BOTH BRITISH AND NORTH AMERICAN BIRDERS, ROSS'S GULL HAS AN ALMOST MYTHICAL STATUS — INDEED ONE BRITISH BIRDER, MICHAEL DENSLEY, DEVOTED AN ENTIRE HARDBACK BOOK TO HIS SEARCH FOR THE SPECIES

In this age of globalisation and a shrinking world, it is salutary to remember that twice a year, one creature continues to travel the entire length of the globe from pole to pole, as it has been doing since time immemorial: the Arctic Tern.

Each year, some of these birds (which weigh less than 120 g) do a round trip of up to 35,000 km between their Arctic breeding grounds and their wintering areas in the Antarctic. A by-product of this epic twice-annual journey is that Arctic Terns experience more hours of daylight than any other animal.

As a global wanderer, it is not surprising that the Arctic Tern shares with the Cattle Egret the honour of being the only species recorded on all seven of the world's continents; and the Arctic Tern is the only bird regularly to occur in (or at least off the coast of) all seven. Its travels are facilitated by a superbly buoyant flight – even by tern standards this species appears extraordinarily graceful. On land, its short legs and long wings – especially when combined with the harsh, grating call – make it rather less attractive.

Like many seabirds, Arctic Terns breed in large, noisy colonies, sometimes comprising several thousand pairs, though the species is also known

Carrying fish to its young – an Arctic Tern in the Farne Islands, England

to nest solitarily in parts of its range. The colonies provide solace for other species too. The terns' notorious aggression – attacking any intruder that comes near their nests by dive-bombing and pecking with that needle-sharp, blood-red bill – attracts more timid species such as Long-tailed Ducks to breed near them as protection against predators. Even so, the Arctic Tern's extreme vulnerability to ground-dwelling mammals such as mink and hedgehogs means that many colonies are found on remote off-shore islands.

Despite all the noise and apparent activity at a tern colony, breeding success at many places is very low, especially on the Shetland Islands off the north of Scotland. This appears to be because of a shortage of the terns' staple food, sand-eels – which in turn is almost certainly due to a rapid increase in sea temperatures caused by global climate change.

One theory is that warmer seas cause the sand-eels to move into deeper waters, and because the terns feed by plunging down from the air to grab food from just beneath the surface, they are unable to catch enough to feed their hungry chicks. Unless they can adapt, and either shift their breeding areas or discover a new diet, the Arctic Tern may soon suffer a major population crash.

ARCTIC TERN | *Sterna paradisaea*

OVER THE COURSE OF A 20-YEAR LIFETIME, A SINGLE ARCTIC TERN MAY TRAVEL AS FAR AS 800,000 KM, MAKING IT THE MOST TRAVELLED CREATURE ON EARTH — IF WE IGNORE HUMAN BEINGS, WHO DO NOT TRAVEL UNDER THEIR OWN STEAM

With its upright gait, comical walk and impossibly colourful bill, it is hardly surprising that the Puffin holds a place as one of our favourite birds. Even people who have never set eyes on a live bird can recognise a picture of an Atlantic Puffin. This is partly – in Britain and the United States at least – due to the adoption of the species in the 1940s as the emblem for Puffin Books, an offshoot of Penguin Books publishing exclusively for children.

Puffins belong to the auk family, the northern-hemisphere equivalent of the penguins, with whom they share a number of characteristics, including the ability to dive and swim underwater for long periods in search of food. Where all auks (apart from the extinct Great Auk) differ from all penguins is, of course, in their ability to fly.

The original name for the species was 'Sea Parrot', though this only lasted for a century or so before the current name was adopted. 'Puffin' was originally given to the salted young of the Manx Shearwater, a delicacy to the 18th-century palate, but confusion between the two species led to it being transferred to the bird we know today.

Like other auks, Puffins are highly social, breeding in dense colonies sometimes numbering tens of thousands of pairs. Unlike their close relatives the guillemots and the razorbills, Puffins do not nest on cliff ledges,

Wings outstretched, the 'sea parrot' or Atlantic Puffin

but prefer the darkness and security of earth burrows. They either dig these themselves, using their powerful feet and claws, or if the opportunity arises they simply take over a burrow from another puffin, shearwater or rabbit.

Being colonial provides many opportunities for encounters between rival males, especially at the start of the breeding season. Conflicts generally take the form of ritualised displays, but fighting does occur, with both males locking their powerful bills together and grappling until one gains the ascendancy.

Like most seabirds, Puffins are long-lived, with a low reproductive rate. They lay a single, whitish egg, which is incubated by either adult for long periods – sometimes more than 24 hours – until their mate returns from feeding out at sea. The young bird remains in the burrow for at least a month, sometimes nearer two; but eventually it either flies or waddles, under cover of darkness, to the sea.

Colonial seabirds are very vulnerable to population declines as a result of both natural and man-made factors. The main natural hazard is winter storms: Puffins spend their time outside the breeding season far out to sea, and may be driven onto coasts or even far inland by heavy winds. In one celebrated occasion, in the 1930s, a Puffin was found walking down the Strand in London, where, not surprisingly, it brought traffic to a standstill.

ATLANTIC PUFFIN | *Fratercula arctica*

LIKE ALL AUKS, PUFFINS ARE FAITHFUL BOTH TO THEIR BREEDING SITE AND TO THEIR MATE: THE 'DIVORCE RATE' AMONGST PUFFINS IS LESS THAN ONE IN FOURTEEN

The fall and rise of the Pink Pigeon – one of nine bird species found only on the island of Mauritius in the Indian Ocean – is a tale of a bird brought back from the brink of extinction; and of both the folly and the goodness of human beings.

Though once widespread throughout the island, by the 19th century the species had been forced out of the lowland areas and into the uplands. Even there, its population continued to decline.

Like its distant relative the Dodo, the Pink Pigeon (the largest of the island's pigeons) evolved to exploit the specialised native vegetation of Mauritius's forests, in an environment free from predators. Despite its large size, it is able to forage for fruit and leaves at the ends of branches, though it also forages on the ground, where its delicate pink underparts and darker upperparts enable it to blend in with the forest floor.

The arrival of European settlers on Mauritius, in the 17th and 18th centuries, was a disaster for these specialised birds. The dogs, cats, pigs and rats the sailors brought with them wreaked havoc on native creatures, while later introductions included the Crab-eating Macaque monkey and Small Indian Mongoose from south-east Asia, both of which are highly efficient at killing pigeons. Deforestation on a massive scale, and the introduction of alien plant species, were also key factors in the species' decline.

Once Critically Endangered, the Mauritius Pink Pigeon has been brought back from the brink of extinction

By the 1950s, the population of Pink Pigeons was down to 40–60 birds; 30 years later, this had fallen to just 20 individuals at a single site, known as Pigeon Wood.

It was then that conservationist Gerald Durrell and his wife Lee began a captive-breeding programme for the Pink Pigeon at his home on the island of Jersey, and in 1984 they released the first batch of pigeons back into the wild. Since then the population has gone from strength to strength: today there are five separate sites with more than 400 wild birds. Durrell wrote about his experiences on Mauritius in his book *Golden Bats and Pink Pigeons.*

However, the situation is still highly precarious. In 2002 numbers at one site plummeted from 100 to just 20 birds – probably as a result both of becoming prey to feral cats and of a parasite reducing breeding success. Conservationists believe that the pigeon population can be maintained only through strict control of potential predators, together with supplementary feeding, as the habitat has become so degraded that the birds are unable to find enough food to support themselves.

So, despite the best efforts of conservationists, the Pink Pigeon is still classified as 'Critically Endangered', and safeguarding its future will require work for many years to come.

MAURITIUS PINK PIGEON | *Nesoenas mayeri*

THE PLIGHT OF THE PINK PIGEON CAME TO THE ATTENTION OF ONE OF THE WORLD'S GREATEST CONSERVATIONISTS, GERALD DURRELL, JUST IN TIME

The Kakapo booms like a bittern, leks like a Black Grouse and lives the nocturnal lifestyle of an owl. No wonder this very rare, flightless bird from New Zealand has been described as one of the most curious birds alive.

With some males weighing in at 3 kg, the Kakapo is by some measure the world's heaviest parrot. It is also one of the world's loudest birds: when trying to attract a female, male Kakapos trample a hollow in the ground which they use as an echo chamber to magnify the volume of their call. As a result, a booming bird can be heard up to 6 km away.

Once found in suitable habitat throughout the North and South Islands, the Kakapo was so common that one 19th-century explorer wrote that 'birds used to be in dozens round the camp, screeching and yelling like a lot of demons, and at times it was impossible to sleep for the noise … on moonlight nights you could shake a tree and the Kakapo would fall down like apples.'

Despite its apparent abundance, the Kakapo went into a sharp decline almost as soon as European settlers arrived in New Zealand. Its large size and inability to fly away made it easy prey for hungry sailors, who found the bird's white flesh very tasty. The usual introduced predators also wreaked havoc on this slow, rather clumsy bird, and like the Dodo it fell victim to Black Rats, though Stoats were also a major predator.

By the end of the 19th century, the Kakapo had become extinct in North Island. Eighty years later, it had also disappeared from South Island, and was confined to the much smaller Stewart Island, at the southern tip of the country. Threatened with imminent extinction by feral cats, between 1987 and 1992 the entire population of Kakapos – numbering just 37 in all – was captured by the New Zealand Wildlife Service and relocated to three tiny offshore islands where it had not formerly been found. As a result, the species became extinct in its natural range.

Its diet includes nuts, seeds and berries, roots and tubers, rhizomes, ferns and fungi. One particular plant is crucial to breeding success: in autumn a good crop of seeds from *Podocarpus*, a type of evergreen conifer, appears to stimulate the parrots to breed. In bad years, they do not even attempt to breed the following spring.

Today, despite the best efforts of conservationists, numbers have risen only very slowly to about 90 birds. Unfortunately the genetic diversity of the population is very low, and many of the females are past breeding age. In a last desperate attempt to kick-start the Kakapo's recovery, scientists are now resorting to collecting sperm from the oldest birds in the hope that the parrots can be bred in the future using artificial insemination techniques.

Nocturnal, rare and flightless, the Kakapo in search of berries

Strigops habroptilus | # KAKAPO

FOR SUCH A RARE BIRD, THE KAKAPO IS SURPRISINGLY UNSPECIALISED WHEN IT COMES TO FEEDING, THOUGH IT IS EXCLUSIVELY VEGETARIAN, EVEN FEEDING VERY YOUNG CHICKS ON PLANT FOOD

Hyacinth Macaws are a stunning sight as they fly in pairs or small flocks across the landscape of the Brazilian Pantanal, their long, narrow wings and tail giving them a very distinctive appearance. It is sad that some people would prefer to see this majestic and beautiful bird cooped up in a cage, rather than flying free.

For although habitat loss is a constant problem for tropical birds, by far the greatest threat to these beautiful parrots is illegal trapping for the cagebird trade. From 1970 to 1990 the wild population declined dramatically, with an estimated 10,000 individuals being captured in a single decade, the 1980s.

The largest of the world's 330 or so species of parrot, it is a rich cobalt-blue in colour, with yellow around the eye and bill. The bill itself is huge, appearing as big as the bird's head, and can exert enormous pressure. This enables the macaws to crush the tough shells of palm nuts in order to extract their tasty kernels – a source of food inaccessible to other birds.

Hyacinth Macaws often seek out burned areas, where the nuts have split open with the heat, making them easier to eat. Unfortunately, trappers sometimes deliberately burn an area to entice the birds into baited traps, where they are caught.

A stunning Hyacinth Macaw at its tree-hole nest in Brazil

Along with the vast majority of parrots, Hyacinth Macaws normally nest in holes in trees, but they will also do so in natural crevices in cliff faces. In recent years, nesting on cliffs appears to have become more common, possibly because there the birds are less vulnerable to trappers, who cut down the nesting tree to reach the chicks.

The chicks themselves are born blind, only gaining their sight after two weeks and their first feathers soon afterwards. The young fledge about three months after hatching, although in most of the documented cases only one of the two chicks survives.

As a result of the unwelcome attention they receive from humans, Hyacinth Macaws are wary birds. They spend most of their time not in dense rainforest, but ranging across lightly wooded country, where stands of trees are interspersed with areas of more open, savannah-type grassland, as well as flooded, swampy areas. Their main stronghold is in the seasonally flooded grasslands of the Mato Grosso in Brazil, though their range also extends into Paraguay and Bolivia.

Today, as few as 3,000 Hyacinth Macaws survive in the wild. Sadly, without urgent and immediate action to stop the illegal trade in wild parrots, the species is a prime candidate for extinction within the next few years.

HYACINTH MACAW | *Anodorhynchus hyacinthinus*

IN A FAMILY CONTAINING MANY STRIKING SPECIES, THE HYACINTH MACAW HAS A GOOD CLAIM TO BEING THE MOST IMPRESSIVE

When the early European explorers of equatorial Africa first cast eyes on the Great Blue Turaco, they must have thought they were seeing things. The largest of the 23 species of turaco, a sub-Saharan family also known in southern Africa as louries, the Great Blue is also the most widespread. It can be found across a broad belt of West and Central Africa, from the Atlantic coast to the Kakamega Forest of western Kenya. This is mainly because the species has a more catholic choice of habitat than other turacos: it is able to live in many different types of forest, including more open savannah-type areas, and can even survive in relict patches provided it is not disturbed or hunted.

Turacos have long been considered to be related to the cuckoos, though they have several features that suggest they really belong in their own order. Turacos are 'semi-zygodactylous', meaning that they have two toes pointing forward, one toe pointing back, while the fourth can be positioned either forward or back. This arrangement of toes enables them to clamber around the branches of trees with great agility. Despite its large size and weight (females may be 75 cm long and weigh over 1 kg), the Great Blue Turaco is able to reach fruit at the tips of thin branches, thanks to its advanced climbing ability.

The feathers on the head and breast of turacos lack the barbules found in most other birds, giving them a soft, delicate appearance, as if covered with a fine layer of hair or fur. But the turacos' truly unique characteristic is also contained in its plumage: two copper pigments that create extraordinary colours. Known as turacin and turacoverdin, these are not found in any other bird or, indeed, in any other animal. In the Great Blue Turaco, turacoverdin gives the green colour to the wings, though in this species the red pigment turacin is absent.

Turacos obtain the copper to make these pigments from a diet consisting mainly of fruit, though the Great Blue also feeds on leaves, which it regurgitates to feed its chicks. Great Blue Turaco nests are vulnerable to predators such as monkeys and snakes, including the Forest Cobra. The young may continue to be fed by the parents for up to three months after they have left the nest.

The striking appearance and beautiful colours of the turacos have made them vulnerable to hunting: both for their feathers (used in head-dresses) and for food. For such a brightly coloured bird, they apparently taste good – according to the African explorer and ornithologist Levaillant they are much better than guinea-fowl.

The striking appearance and beautiful plumage of Africa's Great Blue Turaco

Corythaeola cristata | # GREAT BLUE TURACO

WITH ITS COBALT-BLUE PLUMAGE, RAISED CREST AND BIZARRE BI-COLOURED BILL, THE GREAT BLUE TURACO IS ONE OF THE MOST STRIKING OF ALL AFRICAN BIRDS

Sumer is icumen in
Lhude sing cuccu!

This anonymous rhyme, dating back to the 13th century, is the first mention in English of a familiar bird whose name, of course, represents its call. The name was undoubtedly in use before then, though it is thought to have been brought to Britain by the Normans; Anglo-Saxons preferred the terse and monosyllabic 'gowk'.

Whatever it is called, the Common Cuckoo has a central place in European folklore. It is widely regarded as the harbinger of spring and traditional arrival dates are marked with celebratory 'cuckoo festivals': from 21 March in the south of France, through 14–21 April in Britain, to 1 May in Norway.

The reason the Cuckoo is so celebrated is the bird's highly unusual breeding habits. The Cuckoo is the best-known of the tiny minority of birds (about 100 of the world's total of about 10,000 bird species) that practise a very unusual strategy known as brood parasitism. Instead of building her own nest and raising her young, the female Cuckoo lays her eggs in the nest of another bird, known as the host species. When the chick hatches, it ejects any unhatched eggs or chicks, and is fed and raised entirely by the unsuspecting hosts.

The most famous bird to practise brood parasitism – the Common Cuckoo

Various species are habitual hosts of the Cuckoo: in Britain and northwest Europe the most frequent are Reed Warbler, Dunnock and Meadow Pipit – the latter has earned itself the folk name 'gowk's fool' in northern England for being so gullible. Across the whole of the Cuckoo's vast range, from Ireland in the west to Kamchatka and Japan in the east, more than a hundred different species have acted as hosts.

But why, with the huge size difference between the Cuckoo's egg and chick, and those of its host species, does the parent not suspect something? In fact, both the parasite and the host are engaged in the biological equivalent of an arms race; each side must constantly refine its tactics in order to win. So over generations the Cuckoo has evolved a technique of egg-mimicry, as a result of which its egg is remarkably similar in colour and shape (though not of course size) to that of its hosts. Once the egg hatches, the 'super-stimulus' provided by a giant chick impels the host parents to keep on feeding.

One of the most extraordinary things about the Cuckoo is that having fledged and left the nest sometime in June or July, the young bird is able to fly all the way to sub-Saharan Africa without any guidance from its parents. The following spring it returns, often to the area where it was born, to begin the cycle of parasitism all over again.

COMMON CUCKOO | *Cuculus canorus*

THE NUMBER OF REPETITIONS OF THE CUCKOO'S CALL IS SUPPOSED TO REPRESENT THE NUMBER OF YEARS UNTIL YOU MARRY, THE NUMBER OF CHILDREN YOU WILL HAVE OR THE NUMBER OF YEARS UNTIL YOU DIE, DEPENDING ON YOUR OUTLOOK

'Beep beep!' Along with Donald Duck and Tweety Pie, one North American species of bird has achieved iconic status. This is due to a series of Warner Brothers' cartoons which have delighted generations of children around the world since they first appeared in the late 1940s. The premise behind these cartoons is simple: a character named Wile E. Coyote pursues a bird called the Road Runner, but despite fiendishly complicated and cunning attempts never quite manages to catch him. The cartoon's creator, Chuck Jones (also the mastermind behind Bugs Bunny) based the idea on a travel book by Mark Twain, in which he observed that hungry coyotes sometimes chase roadrunners.

In a clever touch of ornithological humour, the start of each chase sequence in the cartoon is prefixed by mock scientific names, including (for the Road Runner) *Accelleratii incredibus*, *Hot-Roddicus supersonicus*, and, in a cruel tease for the coyote, *Birdius tastius*.

The character is based on the better-known of the two species in its genus, the Greater Roadrunner. Found in the deserts of the southwestern United States and northern Mexico, the species is known by a number of local names indicating its habitat preferences and habits, including 'chaparral cock', and, in Spanish, *Correcaminos*.

This Greater Roadrunner in California has caught a fast-running lizard

Both species are members of the cuckoo family, and part of a smaller subgroup known as ground-cuckoos. Although they are able to fly, they prefer a terrestrial existence, and as their name suggests tend to run when chasing prey or being pursued by a predator. They feed on a wide range of prey, including beetles, lizards and even snakes. In winter, when animal food is scarce, they forage for seeds and fruits, including the prickly pear cactus, a common and characteristic plant of these arid deserts.

When trying to catch a large reptile such as a rattlesnake, the roadrunner uses a combination of speed, agility and surprise: approaching the snake from behind, it grabs the neck in its powerful bill, then batters the reptile to death against a rock or stone. When pursuing a particularly large snake, two roadrunners sometimes carry out a twin-pronged attack. The male uses his ability to catch fast-running prey such as lizards to impress the female and must bring her a selection of morsels before she will allow him to mate.

Unusually amongst birds, the parents incubate in well-defined shifts, the male by night, with male and female taking turns by day. This is thought to be because the males are heavier, and in better overall condition, than the females, enabling them to cope more easily with the very cold night-time temperatures found in the desert.

GREATER ROADRUNNER | *Geococcyx californianus*

A ROADRUNNER CAN RUN AT SPEEDS OF UP TO 40 KILOMETRES PER HOUR, MAKING IT THE FASTEST RUNNER OF ALL FLYING BIRDS — ONLY THE OSTRICH AND OTHER FLIGHTLESS SPECIES CAN BEAT IT

Once known only to keen birders eager to set eyes on this beautiful Arctic creature, the Snowy Owl now has a wider following, and is loved by children and adults all over the world. The species' new-found fame is entirely due to its appearance in the celebrated *Harry Potter* series of books by J.K. Rowling (and of course the subsequent films), in which Harry's constant companion Hedwig is a Snowy Owl.

In reality, Snowy Owls are creatures of the Arctic tundra, with a classic circumpolar distribution: they breed in Alaska and northern Canada, in Greenland (but not Iceland) and Scandinavia, and in the northern parts of Siberia. However, being a nomadic species, it is prone to wandering south, regularly turning up in the United States (as far south as California, Texas and Florida), and also occasionally in Britain. Vagrants have even been sighted in the Azores and Bermuda, little more than 30 degrees north of the equator.

The Snowy Owl's propensity to wander (technically known as irruption) is directly linked to its food supply. That consists particularly of lemmings and voles, whose populations are highly cyclical. In poor lemming years, Snowy Owls will venture far and wide, sometimes breeding well to the south of their normal range, such as the birds that famously nested on the Shetland island of Fetlar in the late 1960s and 1970s.

In good lemming years, however, Snowy Owls will lay clutches of up to 11 eggs, though between three and five is the more usual number. If the food supply lasts through the summer they may raise all their young; if it fails, most – if not all – will die.

The hunting owl is helped by acute hearing, enabling it to detect the presence of a rustling rodent beneath a layer of snow. In poor lemming and vole years a wide variety of other prey may be taken, including Ptarmigan, Mountain Hares, geese and even beetles.

Snowy Owls are well adapted to life beyond the Arctic Circle, having snow-white plumage (flecked with black in the female and young birds), long, thick feathers, and extensive feathering around the legs and feet. The species plays a key part in the ecology of the Arctic, with wildfowl such as Snow Geese often breeding in the vicinity of an owl's nest and relying on them to warn of approaching predators such as the Arctic Fox. Owls tend to nest in open areas with rocks for use as lookout posts.

The beautiful Arctic sight of a Snowy Owl

Bubo scandiaca | # SNOWY OWL

NOT SURPRISINGLY FOR SUCH A STRIKING AND CHARISMATIC BIRD, THE SNOWY OWL HAS ATTRACTED ITS FAIR SHARE OF FOLKLORE. IN ROMANIA, IT IS BELIEVED THAT THE SOULS OF REPENTANT SINNERS FLY TO HEAVEN IN THE FORM OF SNOWY OWLS

The largest and heaviest of the world's 190 or so species of owl, the Eurasian Eagle-owl is also the most majestic. Standing taller than a buzzard, it is up to three times as heavy: a female can weigh more than 4 kg, making it a fearsome hunter.

Eagle-owls take a very wide range of prey items, including large birds of prey and mammals up to the size of an adult hare. However, the vast majority of their prey items are much smaller, mainly small rodents (voles) and insectivores (shrews) weighing as little as 10 g – revealing the opportunistic nature of their hunting methods.

However, the reputation of the species is such that they have long been persecuted by farmers and gamekeepers throughout Europe, who live in fear for the safety of their lambs. Pesticides are another major threat, especially as the Eagle-owl is at the very top of the food chain, so accumulated residues have a potent effect on their metabolism. During the 1960s and 1970s some populations, especially those around the Mediterranean, suffered badly because of the lack of rabbits caused by the disease myxomatosis.

As a fairly secretive bird of remote, often hilly and wooded areas, the Eagle-owl is more often heard than seen. This explains why in German and Dutch its common names are onomatopoeic representations of the call: *Uhu* and *Oehoe*, respectively. The French prefer to acknowledge the bird's aristocratic appearance: in a nod to their pre-republican days, the species is known as *Grand-duc d'Europe*.

The various races of Eagle-owls found across Europe and Asia are a textbook example of Bergmann's rule, which proposes that individuals of the same species tend to get larger as one gets closer to the North Pole. Eagle-owls found in the deserts of North Africa, the Middle East and Arabia are about 20 per cent shorter and virtually half the weight of their north European counterparts, as well as being much paler in colour; these have now been officially accorded status as a full species, Pharaoh Eagle-owl.

In Britain, Eagle-owls have long held an almost mythical status, with no officially proven records in recent times. However, in the last decade birds that have either escaped or been deliberately released have not only survived in the wild but have successfully bred, raising a number of free-flying young.

The owls' presence has also split the birding community between those who regard the species as a welcome addition (or re-addition) to the British avifauna, and those who consider them an alien invader to be shot on sight. Given that the species probably lived in Britain in historical times, and given its declining status in Europe as a whole, perhaps it should be welcomed rather than shunned.

Coming in to land – the Eurasian Eagle Owl

Bubo bubo | # EURASIAN EAGLE-OWL

THE EAGLE-OWL MAY HAVE INSPIRED ONE OF THE GREAT CLASSICS OF CHILDREN'S LITERATURE, EDWARD LEAR'S 'THE OWL AND THE PUSSYCAT'. LEAR WAS ALSO ONE OF BRITAIN'S GREATEST BIRD ARTISTS

The Oilbird is the world's only nocturnal fruit-eating bird, first discovered by the Prussian explorer and naturalist Alexander von Humboldt in Venezuela in 1799. The bird remained elusive and mysterious for many years afterwards, its bizarre appearance and unique habits baffling ornithologists.

Once thought to be related to owls, and at times linked with trogons, cuckoos and rollers, the species is now considered to be most closely related to the nightjars and their allies. Nevertheless, it differs from them sufficiently – especially in its diet (all other nightjars feed on insects) – to be one of only 23 species of bird in the world to be granted its own, single-species family.

Living in caves, often in remote, inaccessible areas, Oilbirds emerge after dark like fruit bats – which they superficially resemble – in order to feast on the fruit of the oil palm and other tropical plants. Like other nightjar-type birds the Oilbird has long wings, giving it a very agile and graceful flight and enabling it to find its way through the cave systems that are its daytime home. Its tiny feet are only used to cling to vertical surfaces of rock or perch on cave ledges.

Another feature the Oilbird shares with only a few other species, notably the cave-swiftlets of Asia,

The nocturnal, cave-dwelling Oilbird on its nest in Trinidad

is the ability to use echolocation to find its way around caves in the darkness. However, this is nowhere near as complex or sophisticated as the system used by bats, and uses frequencies audible to the human ear – a series of sharp clicking sounds. It also emits blood-curdling, high-pitched screams, as a result of which it is believed that the Oilbird's caves are the resting places for tormented souls.

The Oilbird is one of the classic target species for birders visiting any part of its range, from Trinidad and Panama south through Colombia, Venezuela and Guyana to Brazil, Ecuador, Bolivia and Peru. In one case this resulted in tragedy, when two British birders searching for Oilbirds were captured and killed by the Shining Path guerrillas of Peru.

Both the Oilbird's English and scientific names refer to the custom of taking Oilbird chicks and cooking them to extract oil for cooking and lighting. The chicks may be twice as heavy as the parent birds due to their extensive fat deposits.

Harvesting the chicks is not a pleasant business, as the floors of the Oilbird's caves are generally covered with hordes of invertebrates, including spiders, scorpions and cockroaches. Oilbirds also regurgitate seeds, which form mounds up to 3 m high. It is not clear whether the harvesting affects Oilbird numbers, though the species is known to be very vulnerable to disturbance, and colonies may permanently desert their caves if they are visited too regularly.

OILBIRD | *Steatornis caripensis*

OILBIRDS ARE HIGHLY SOCIAL AND GREGARIOUS, WITH UP TO 10,000 BIRDS BREEDING IN A SINGLE COLONY

Watching Swifts as they sweep across the suburban skyline, it is hard to imagine that once they leave Europe, some of these birds will not touch down again for almost two whole years, having been to Africa and back – twice! Yet once young Swifts leave the safety of their nest, they will perform just such a feat, flying countless thousands of miles, and feeding, sleeping and even mating on the wing.

Swifts are remarkable in many other ways, too. Because they depend entirely on small flying insects, which are scarce during prolonged and heavy rain, the young are able to go into a form of torpor approaching a state of hibernation, for several days or even weeks if necessary. Meanwhile, their parents may fly several hundred kilometres away from the nest, skirting around the edge of a weather front until it has finally passed and they are able to return.

The Common Swift's scientific name, *Apus apus*, literally means 'without feet'. Although the species does of course possess feet, they are so small and rudimentary that they can only be used to cling on to vertical or near-vertical surfaces, such as the walls of buildings where the birds make their nests. Should a Swift be forced to land on the ground – for example if forced down by heavy rain – it is often unable to take off again without human help.

Despite its name, the one thing the Swift is not particularly remarkable for is its speed. In fact it is nowhere near the fastest flying bird, though when you watch a squadron chasing each other at rooftop height they certainly give the impression of speed and pace. In fact, their typical speed is between 23 and 40 km per hour, though their Asiatic relative, the White-throated Needletail, has been recorded at speeds of up to 170 km per hour – which it puts to good use on its 24,000 km round-trip between Siberia and Tasmania.

Another Asian species, the Edible-nest Swiftlet, has a unique place in the economic, gastronomic and cultural life of the people, with the trade in nests (used to make bird's nest soup) worth more than $1 billion (over £520 million) to Indonesia alone.

Common Swifts have a long association with folklore across their breeding range, and – perhaps because of their dark colour and characteristic screaming call – are frequently associated with the Devil. Folk names found in various parts of Britain include Devil Bird, Devil Screech, Devil Swallow and Swing Devil – the last no doubt a reference to the birds' habit of racing low across the skyline in tight, noisy flocks. More affectionate names include Deviling and Dicky Devlin, the latter originating in Yorkshire.

A montage of Common Swifts in flight – they feed, sleep and even mate on the wing

Apus apus | # COMMON SWIFT

ALTOGETHER THERE ARE ALMOST A HUNDRED SPECIES OF SWIFT, FOUND THROUGHOUT THE WORLD APART FROM THE POLAR REGIONS, BUT WITH THE HIGHEST CONCENTRATION OF SPECIES IN THE TROPICS

All the world's 330 or so species of hummingbird are remarkable: no other birds have evolved the ability to fly in any direction – including up, down and backwards – at will. They have done so in order to take advantage of the energy-rich nectar produced by flowers – nectar that, although accessible to insects, is usually difficult for birds to obtain.

In order to exploit this rich source of food, many hummingbirds have evolved long, sometimes decurved, bills, which they insert into the flowers of tropical plants. But the champion of them all is the Sword-billed Hummingbird of the Andes.

The bill of this aptly named species can measure between 9 and 11 cm – sometimes more than half the bird's total body-length – giving it a bizarre, front-heavy appearance. Indeed, at first sight the bird looks as if it is carrying some sort of weapon in front of it, an impression which undoubtedly led to the French and Spanish names *colibri porte-epée* and *colibri picoespada* – both references to the sport of fencing. When the bird perches, it must tilt its head back to prevent it from toppling over.

Unusually amongst hummingbirds, whose bills are almost always straight or decurved, the bill of this species has a pronounced upward tilt, especially towards the tip, which may enable it to gain an advantage

The hugely long, upward tilting bill of the Sword-billed Hummingbird in the Andes Mountains, Ecuador

when probing into the flowers on which it feeds. These tend to have long, pendent corollas, and because of their length are rarely visited by other hummingbirds, giving the Sword-billed a competitive advantage when it comes to finding food.

Like other members of its family, the Sword-billed Hummingbird hawks for insects, feeding on the wing in the manner of a swift or swallow, snapping its bill shut as soon as it makes contact with its prey.

The Sword-billed Hummingbird is found in humid, montane forest and its edges, along the northern part of the Andes mountain range: from western Venezuela, through Colombia, Ecuador and Peru to northeast Bolivia. Like many species of hummingbird, it is largely sedentary, but in Colombia it can be found during the summer months at altitudes of 3,000 to 3,500 m. Other than its extraordinary bill, it is not a particularly unusual-looking bird, with the iridescent green plumage common to many of its family.

With its reasonably large range and montane habitat, the Sword-billed Hummingbird is not considered threatened, though it may not be quite so widespread as it once was: at the beginning of the 20th century it was considered common around the suburbs of the capital of Ecuador, Quito. Its extraordinary appearance makes it an ideal species to use to attract eco-tourists and birders, so helping to prevent the destruction of its precious habitat.

SWORD-BILLED HUMMINGBIRD | *Ensifera ensifera*

Few other species can boast such a combination of great beauty, religious and cultural significance, and allure for birders visiting their Central American home. Even the name 'quetzal' itself means 'precious' or 'beautiful'.

The Resplendent Quetzal is the best-known member of the trogon family, a group of almost 40 long-tailed, brightly coloured birds found in tropical America, Africa and Asia. What marks out this particular species from its relatives is the extraordinarily long tail of the male, whose two central plumes may extend as much as 65 cm beyond the rest – making up almost two-thirds of its total body-length.

Its allure is further heightened by the fact that its range is not only relatively small, but covers some of the world's more inaccessible (and often dangerous) places: from the Oaxaca and Chiapas provinces of southern Mexico, through Guatemala, Honduras, El Salvador and Nicaragua, to Panama. Only in Costa Rica, where the bird is relatively common despite being hunted for its plumes until the 1970s, can it be looked for in relative safety and comfort. Throughout its range, it lives in evergreen montane forest, usually from 900 to 3,200 m above sea level.

The Resplendent Quetzal is classed as 'Near-threatened' currently rather than as

The tail feathers of the Resplendent Quetzal make up almost two-thirds of the bird's entire body length

endangered, but remains under constant threat from hunting and in particular habitat loss: not only is deforestation fragmenting its habitat, but global climate change may also have serious effects. The quetzal's situation is not helped by the extraordinarily high mortality rate of its chicks, of which about 80 per cent die before fledging; and another 80 per cent perish before they reach adulthood.

Sacred to both the Mayan and Aztec peoples, the bird gave its name to the Aztec god Quetzalcoatl, symbolised by the head of a serpent adorned with quetzal feathers. As a result of its link with the deity, the penalty for killing a quetzal was death; so the birds were often caught and had their tail-feathers removed before being released.

When the Spanish *conquistador* Hernan Cortes arrived in Mexico in 1519, the Aztec leader Montezuma sent him a head-dress of quetzal plumes, signifying a widespread belief that Cortes and the men who accompanied him were returning gods. Unfortunately for the peoples of Mexico, this could not have been further from the truth.

Today, the Resplendent Quetzal is the national bird of Guatemala, and even the country's currency is named after it. It was celebrated by the American writer Jonathan Evan Maslow in his travelogue *Bird of Life, Bird of Death*, in which its rapid and serious decline was contrasted with the success of the scavenging 'bird of death', the American Black Vulture.

RESPLENDENT QUETZAL | *Pharomachrus mocinno*

OF ALL THE WORLD'S BIRDS, THE WONDERFULLY NAMED RESPLENDENT QUETZAL IS PERHAPS THE MOST TRULY REMARKABLE

A bird that laughs like a clown, wrestles snakes more than twice its length, and has one of the most highly developed cooperative breeding strategies in the avian kingdom, deserves respect.

Despite its preference for relatively dry habitats, the Laughing Kookaburra is a member of the kingfisher family. It competes with Africa's Giant Kingfisher for the title of the largest of the 90 or so species – being heavier, though marginally shorter, than its rival.

The Laughing Kookaburra is native to much of eastern Australia, from the northern tip of Queensland south to Victoria, New South Wales and the eastern parts of South Australia. In the late 19th century the species was introduced to the south-western tip of Western Australia and Tasmania. The Governor of New Zealand, Sir George Grey, also brought Kookaburras to his private retreat on Kawau Island, off New Zealand's North Island, where they still live today.

The name 'kookaburra' – also given to three other species of the genus *Dacelo* found in New Guinea and northern Australia – derives from one of the now-extinct aboriginal languages of Australia, and is representative of the species' laughing call. It is this maniacal sound which has brought the Kookaburra fame throughout the world: indeed, the species was one of three typically Australian creatures to be chosen as mascots for the 2000 Sydney Olympics – the others being the Echidna and the Duck-billed Platypus. The call is usually uttered in chorus by a flock of birds, one starting off, and the others joining in, to create a cacophony of hysterical laughter.

But the laughing call has a far more important function than simply entertaining visitors to the Australian bush. Kookaburras live in family units of half-a-dozen or so birds, and like other species (including some bee-eaters, wood-hoopoes and babblers) have evolved a complex breeding strategy: younger, non-breeding relatives help the adults care for the young. Interestingly, where the 'helpers' are male birds the pair tends to produce more female offspring, and vice versa. Despite this familial loyalty, when food is scarce Kookaburra chicks will fight to the death, with the larger chicks killing their younger siblings.

One of the Kookaburra's most remarkable features is its ability to capture large snakes – up to a metre in length. It does so by grabbing the reptile behind the head, then bashing it violently against a tree branch or on the ground in order to stun it, before finally swallowing it whole.

A Kookaburra laughing – this ability has made it a mascot in Australia

Dacelo novaeguineae | # LAUGHING KOOKABURRA

DUE TO ITS RATHER COMICAL APPEARANCE AND ENDEARING HABITS, THE LAUGHING KOOKABURRA IS REGARDED MORE WITH AFFECTION THAN ADMIRATION — THOUGH AMONGST AUSTRALIANS IT IS NO LESS POPULAR FOR THAT

Long a favourite amongst birders, writers and the general public alike, the Common Kingfisher is one of the Old World's most iconic but least observed birds. As one observer put it, 'only the righteous ever see the Kingfisher'. This is especially true in Europe and southern Asia, where, although it is widespread and locally common, due to its secretive habits it is often surprisingly hard to see.

Indeed, the first clue to its presence is usually the high-pitched, repetitive call, often given in flight, followed by a flash of brilliant blue and orange as the bird zips past. When they finally see it properly, perched on a twig or branch above the water, most people remark how tiny the bird appears: barely larger than a sparrow. Yet despite its small size it glows with an almost luminous blue and orange, assaulting the observer's retina with its colours.

Its fame has, paradoxically, led to a dearth of local or folk names for this celebrated bird. Folklore expert Francesca Greenoak discovered only two British alternatives, 'fisher' (Yorkshire) and 'dipper' (Shropshire) – the latter clearly confusable with the other waterbird bearing that name. It seems that 'fisher' was the standard name for the species until the time of the English Civil War, when – perhaps in an act of support for deposed monarch Charles I, the preface 'king's' was added. A more ancient name, 'isern', derives from an Old English term meaning 'iron-coloured', though whether this refers to the electric-blue upperparts or rusty-orange underparts is a matter for debate.

Like all birds that live alongside, and depend on, fresh water, the Kingfisher is especially sensitive to two threats: pollution, and spells of harsh winter weather. Fortunately, at least in western Europe, rivers are cleaner than they have been for a long time, allowing the species to thrive without the danger of poisoning by chemicals. The same is not always true in the developing world, where increasing industrialisation and the resulting pollution of rivers and streams may threaten this jewel of a bird.

Long, hard winters are also a thing of the past across much of the Common Kingfisher's European range. The impact of the famous 'Big Freeze' of 1962/63, which reduced Britain's Kingfisher population by more than 90 per cent in a single winter, is now but a distant memory. Nowadays, with rivers and streams rarely icing over as they used to, Kingfishers are able to catch fish all year round. Nor are they hunted as they were in Victorian times, when every country house had a glass case filled with trophies, the centrepiece of which would often be a stuffed and mounted Kingfisher.

Most people only see a flash of blue and orange as a Common Kingfisher flies past

Alcedo atthis | # COMMON KINGFISHER

A BIRD THAT TRULY LIVES UP TO ITS NAME AS THE ANGLER EXTRAORDINAIRE OF THE BIRD WORLD, THE COMMON KINGFISHER IS THE BEST KNOWN OF ALMOST ONE HUNDRED MEMBERS OF ITS FAMILY

One of the best-known birds of the Caribbean, Central America and the northern half of South America, the Blue-crowned Motmot is also one of the most striking. With its bright green plumage, multi-coloured head pattern and extra-ordinarily long tail (about half its total body length) it superficially resembles its closest relatives, the bee-eaters of the Old World. However, the ten species of motmots are exclusively found in the Neotropics.

The Blue-crowned Motmot's most extraordinary feature, shared with most of its family, is the unique shape of its tail. The length is accentuated by the fact that the two central feathers are longer than the rest, and have a portion of their shaft bare of feathering, culminating in two racquet-shaped tips. It is not known exactly why this peculiar feature evolved, but it is likely to be used for signalling between male and female during courtship.

Several South American tribes have used motmot feathers for ornamental purposes, while folklore from the Pareci tribe of Brazil's Mato Grosso suggests that the gaps in the motmot's tail were produced by the bird carrying fiery embers. The species was well known to the Maya civilisation of Central America, and can still be seen amongst the ruined Mayan temples of Tikal in Guatemala and Palenque in Mexico.

The unique tail of the Blue-crowned Motmot is clear as it sits on a branch in Tobago

For such brightly coloured birds, motmots are surprisingly inconspicuous, often perching motionless for hours on end, either on a shady perch or occasionally in full sun. They feed by flying off their perch and seizing their insect prey from the branches of a tree, or by dropping to the ground and foraging amongst the leaf-litter.

The Blue-crowned Motmot's large, powerful bill is well suited to taking larger insects such as beetles, as well as snails, centipedes and lizards, which it has been known to chase across the forest floor. Once caught, larger prey such as frogs may be beaten to death on a twig or branch before being consumed.

Fruit – especially nutmegs – are an important component of the motmot's diet; and they will also follow hordes of army ants, taking any small creatures disturbed by their progress.

Like their close relatives the bee-eaters and kingfishers, Blue-crowned Motmots nest in a tunnel dug into an earth bank, sometimes concealed behind a tree root or stump. The female lays her clutch of three or four almost spherical, white eggs in a chamber at the far end – keeping them safe from predators such as mammals and reptiles. The young are born bare and helpless, and their unsanitary habits mean that despite the effort involved, their parents must dig a new burrow each year, the old one having become a serious health hazard!

BLUE-CROWNED MOTMOT | *Momotus momota*

ON THE TOURIST ISLAND OF TOBAGO MOTMOTS REGULARLY VISIT HOTEL BALCONIES FOR AFTERNOON TEA, TAKING A RANGE OF UNSUITABLE ITEMS INCLUDING CAKES AND SANDWICHES

The 25 species of bee-eater are, collectively, one of the most beautiful of all our bird families. Together they have evolved the extraordinary behaviour that gives the group its name: they catch, kill and eat some of the world's most venomous insects, bees and wasps. They have also developed other fascinating adaptations, including co-operative breeding by family groups.

Of all the world's bee-eaters, most of which are found in Africa or Asia, the most widespread and well-known is undoubtedly the European Bee-eater. It is the only member of its family to have extended its range northwards into Europe, with virtually the whole of its breeding area lying outside the equatorial and tropical regions.

Curiously, as well as breeding across a wide swathe of southern Europe and western Asia, the species also breeds in southern Africa. European Bee-eaters are highly migratory, with the northern populations travelling in large, noisy flocks to winter in sub-Saharan Africa – in a narrow strip across the Sahel zone in West Africa, and across a large area south of the equator.

Bee-eaters are capable of taking any insect between 5 mm and 50 mm in length, each item caught on the wing in an impressive display of aerobatics. Because their diet consists entirely of these insects, they rarely need to drink, obtaining all the liquid refreshment they need from their food.

One question often asked about bee-eaters is how they manage not to get stung; or if they *are* stung, how they minimise the effects of the poison. In fact the bee-eater is no more immune to the effects of a bee-sting than any other creature. So, once caught, each stinging insect not only has to be immobilised (achieved by bashing it against a tree branch or other hard surface), but 'devenomed' – rubbed vigorously until both the sting and the venom are removed, and the prey can be swallowed.

How a bee-eater knows which insects are venomous and which are not remains a mystery, but studies have shown that this behaviour in young birds is instinctive rather than taught by their parents.

Bee-eaters are sociable birds, usually breeding in small colonies. Like their relatives the kingfishers, rollers and motmots, they nest in holes, which are usually dug into the side of a sandbank. This is a difficult process, taking up to three weeks, and resulting in the bird's bill becoming about 2 mm shorter than it was when it started! In spring, overshooting birds have been known to breed well to the north of their normal areas, also enabling them to extend their range at times of climatic warming.

The glorious colours of a pair of European Bee-eaters in Spain

Merops apiaster | # EUROPEAN BEE-EATER

DESPITE ITS NAME, THE EUROPEAN BEE-EATER DOES NOT FEED EXCLUSIVELY ON BEES, THOUGH IN EUROPE ITS MAIN PREY DOES CONSIST OF BUMBLEBEES AND HONEYBEES

The rollers, like their close relatives the bee-eaters and kingfishers, are amongst the most colourful of birds. And of the dozen species of roller, the prize for the most stunning goes, by a narrow margin, to the Lilac-breasted Roller of southern and eastern Africa.

This species has a predominantly azure-blue plumage, especially noticeable in the flashes of blue in its wings when the bird takes to the air. It shares with its close cousin, the Abyssinian Roller, two elongated tail-streamers, extending up to 8 cm beyond the rest of its tail. But unlike any of its relatives, this bird also sports a vivid, lilac-coloured breast, which gives the species its name.

The Lilac-breasted Roller is fairly common and widespread across a wide swathe of sub-Saharan Africa, from Eritrea and Somalia in the north to the northern part of South Africa in the south, and from Angola in the west to the Kenyan coast in the east.

It prefers a savannah habitat, with acacia trees on which it can perch; but it also lives in pure grassland areas, where it uses any raised object, including rocks, small bushes or man-made objects such as fences and telegraph wires, to survey its territory.

Like other rollers, the Lilac-breasted feeds by plunging down from these high points to grab an unwary insect – with locusts, crickets and grasshoppers all favourite items of prey. However, as an opportunistic feeder it will also take a wide range of food items including lizards, small birds and frogs. Its bill has the characteristic hooked tip common to all its close relatives, useful for seizing small items of prey. The roller will subdue its prey by bashing it repeatedly against a hard surface, then swallow it whole – a process which in the case of some of its larger food items may take several minutes.

Lilac-breasted Rollers also indulge in a process known as 'courtship feeding', in which the male will present items of prey to his mate. As well as strengthening the pair bond, this is thought to allow the female to save her energy for egg-laying rather than catching her own food.

Like other rollers, the Lilac-breasted has a light, buoyant flight; and like the eight other members of its genus *Coracias* it indulges in the famous 'rolling' courtship display: an acrobatic series of twists, turns and rolls performed during a conspicuous exhibition flight. Contrary to popular belief, however, the bird does not in fact roll through a full 360-degree turn; instead it keeps its head level (presumably to avoid becoming disorientated) while rapidly rotating its body and wings from side to side.

The stunning colour of the Lilac-breasted Roller, perched on a branch in Botswana

LILAC-BREASTED ROLLER | *Coracias caudatus*

THE LILAC-BREASTED ROLLER IS SO STUNNING THAT TOURIST GROUPS IN SEARCH OF BIG CATS IN KENYA'S MASAI MARA HAVE BEEN KNOWN, WHEN CONFRONTED BY CLOSE-UP VIEWS OF THIS GORGEOUS CREATURE, TO IGNORE THEIR FELINE QUARRY

Appearances can be deceptive, especially in the bird world, but rarely can there have been quite such a gulf between beauty and behaviour as in the Hoopoe. When nesting, their sanitary regime has to be smelled to be believed. Once the birds have chosen their home – usually in a hole in a tree or crevice inside a wall – the female produces a fluid with a stench like rotting meat, which not surprisingly acts as a highly effective deterrent to predators. From the sixth day after hatching, the chicks themselves can squirt liquid faeces at any intruder.

Despite these unsavoury habits, the Hoopoe was revered in Ancient Egypt, and its image is preserved in hieroglyphs on royal tombs. It is also featured in the works of authors from Aristophanes to Salman Rushdie – Rushdie used the bird to signify the spirit of a dead king in his book *Haroun and the Sea of Stories*.

The instant-recognisability factor of the Hoopoe is one explanation for its fame. No other bird in the world sports the Hoopoe's unique combination of orangey-buff plumage, a raised crest and black-and-white wings, giving it the appearance of a giant butterfly as it takes to the air.

Found throughout southern Europe and in parts of Africa and Asia, the Hoopoe is migratory in parts of its range while sedentary in others; thus in parts of Africa both the European and African races can be seen side by side – the African race having a more orange plumage.

The Hoopoe gets both its English and scientific names from its piping call, produced when the singing male inclines his head downwards and inflates his neck, before releasing the air in a double-noted sound. It would be easy to assume that the crest is also used for courtship purposes but, in fact, it appears to be employed to deter predators. Indeed, Hoopoes are rarely eaten, possibly as a result of frightening any would-be foe, but more likely because their flesh is, apparently, highly distasteful.

Hoopoes use their long, narrow, and slightly decurved bills to probe for food just below the surface of soil. They feed on a wide range of invertebrates, as well as on smaller vertebrates such as lizards and frogs, which are swiftly grabbed and dispatched. The species is known to prey on many insects that are agricultural pests, making it popular throughout its range, especially amongst farmers. As a result, nest boxes are frequently provided for Hoopoes, despite the disgusting odour associated with breeding birds.

The Hoopoe has an instantly recognisable crest

Upupa epops | # HOOPOE

HOOPOES ARE AMONGST A SELECT GROUP OF BIRDS THAT INDULGE IN A BEHAVIOUR KNOWN AS 'DUST-BATHING' — A PROCESS BY WHICH THE BIRD CLEANSES THE GREASE FROM ITS PLUMAGE BY WRIGGLING ITS FEATHERS IN FINE DUST OR SAND

Some birds have to be seen to be believed – and even then they appear to defy logic. For, of the 50 or so members of the hornbill family, the Rhinoceros Hornbill is not only one of the largest (beaten in size only by the Great and Helmeted Hornbills and the two ground-hornbills), it also boasts the most prominent 'casque' – the horn-like protuberance on top of the bill that gives the family its name.

Uniquely, the casque of the Rhinoceros Hornbill is upturned – resembling the horn of the Asiatic Rhinoceros with which it shares its range. The ivory-coloured bill shades to a deep orange (sometimes virtually blood-red) on the casque – a result of the dyes in the oil the bird uses to preen its feathers. Although females also have a prominent casque, theirs is slightly smaller than that of the male. In both sexes, the bill contrasts dramatically with the matt-black plumage and white vent and tail.

The Rhinoceros Hornbill is confined to southeast Asia, its range extending from Thailand and Malaysia south through the Indonesian islands of Sumatra and Borneo to Java. As a species dependent on primary forest it has suffered from the widespread deforestation of the region, though at present it is not considered endangered, being in the 'Near-threatened' category. Fortunately, like other hornbills, it can live for more than 20 years in the wild.

The unique upturned casque on the bill gives this bird its name

Given its striking appearance, it is not surprising that the Rhinoceros Hornbill plays a large part in the folklore and culture of local people. For the Dayak people of Indonesia, the species represents their god of war. In a traditional ceremony performed at the start of a battle, they carry carved effigies of hornbills, which are used to summon the powers of the war-god against their enemies.

Like other large Asiatic hornbills, the Rhinoceros Hornbill has also been hunted for its feathers and bill, both of which are used in traditional and ceremonial dress. In more recent and enlightened times, the Malaysian state of Sarawak has adopted the species as its state bird.

Hornbills are well known for having some of the most bizarre nesting habits of any bird, and the Rhinoceros Hornbill is no exception. In order to guard against the female being attacked and killed by predators, once she is inside the nest-hole her mate literally walls her in, using mud to seal up the entrance. The female then moults her wing and tail feathers, becoming incapable of flight.

The female will remain in the nest for up to three months, during the entire incubation period and for the first month or more of her chicks' lives. As a result of this unusual strategy, she and her brood are entirely dependent on the male for food; if he should be killed, they will all starve to death.

RHINOCEROS HORNBILL | *Buceros rhinoceros*

EVEN AMONGST THE EXTRAORDINARY FAMILY OF HORNBILLS, THE APPEARANCE OF THE RHINOCEROS HORNBILL IS REMARKABLE

In 1935, graphic artist John Gilroy and advertising copywriter Dorothy L. Sayers (later to become a bestselling mystery novelist) were commissioned to create a campaign for a well-known brand of Irish beer. In a stroke of genius, Gilroy depicted a large, colourful toucan, while Sayers composed the memorable verse:

If he can say as you can
Guinness is good for you,
How grand to be a Toucan,
Just think what Toucan do.

This punning verse established forever the connection between this fruit-eating bird of the South American rainforest and the Guinness brand. Later campaigns explored other, often rather avant-garde territory, but the toucan remains among the most famous of all its incarnations. The toucan also appears in a wide range of other cultural output, and is a particular favourite amongst children's authors and illustrators.

The fame of this, the largest of the world's 34 species of toucan, comes from its extraordinary multi-coloured bill. This truly is a miracle of evolution: despite its huge size – 20 by 8 cm – it is very light, enabling the bird to fly and climb without hindrance. The bill evolved to take advantage of the abundant fruit supplies in the bird's woodland home; despite its bulk, the toucan can use it to manipulate a wide range of different-sized fruits. However, the Toco Toucan is not averse to augmenting its fruit-based diet with insects such as caterpillars, and even with eggs stolen from other birds' nests.

As with other toucans, the Toco is a sociable bird, often foraging in small parties. However, during the breeding season it becomes highly territorial; pairs in captivity have even been known to gang up on a third bird and kill it.

Like other hole-nesters, their eggs are pure white (having no need for camouflage). The young are born naked and blind, and stay in the nest for up to eight weeks after hatching, dependent on their parents for food.

The Toco Toucan's range extends across much of central South America, though its main stronghold is Brazil, where it is found across a wide area including the Amazon basin and the Mato Grosso. It has a more catholic choice of habitat, and lives in more open habitats, than many of its relatives, including woodland edges and even suburban gardens. Although not globally threatened, as a favourite of the pet trade the species is in constant demand. Its inquisitive nature means that it will readily respond to calls and whistles, and is easily captured.

The extraordinary multi-coloured bill of the Toco Toucan has made it world famous

Ramphastos toco | # TOCO TOUCAN

TOUCANS ARE VERY AGILE CLIMBERS, ABLE TO HANG UPSIDE DOWN AND MANOEUVRE THEIR BILLS FROM SIDE TO SIDE IN ORDER TO OBTAIN THEIR FAVOURITE FOOD OF FIGS

The world's 200 or so species of woodpecker are a diverse bunch: having split from their closest relatives more than 50 million years ago, they have had plenty of opportunity to exploit a wide range of ecological niches. Even so, the two species of wryneck are about as different from other woodpeckers as it is possible to be while still being in the same family.

Of the two, the Eurasian or Northern Wryneck has by far the wider distribution, its breeding range extending widely over Europe and Asia, from Portugal in the west to Japan in the east. Eurasian Wrynecks winter in southern Asia and central Africa, sharing part of their African range with the Red-throated (or Rufous-necked) Wryneck.

Although they nest in tree-holes, wrynecks lack the stiff tail and specialised arrangement of toes evolved by other woodpeckers to climb trees, so they are able to forage for food (mainly ants) on open areas of grass.

Wrynecks also lack the ability to make their own nest-holes, so must compete with species such as starlings, Jackdaws and Stock Doves to take over an existing hole or cavity in the trunk of a tree.

Again, unlike other woodpeckers, wrynecks lay large clutches: sometimes as many as a dozen eggs in a single nest. As a result, both adults must work extremely

At home on the ground – the Eurasian Wryneck

hard when the chicks have hatched, bringing food items and carrying away faecal sacs constantly during the three weeks the young remain in the nest. Once the chicks have fledged, their parents' work is far from over: they will continue to feed their offspring for up to two weeks afterwards.

Wrynecks have an extraordinary way of defending their nests against potential predators. As the intruder approaches, the Wryneck puts its head out of the hole and twists its neck, making a hissing sound that presumably fools the creature into believing that a snake is in residence. The 19th-century poet John Clare used this as the basis for a poem, 'The Wryneck's Nest', in which a boy attempting to take the bird's eggs gets a nasty shock!

Sadly, since Clare's day the Eurasian Wryneck has gone from being a widespread and familiar part of the English avifauna to extinction as a British breeding bird – one of only a handful of species to become extinct in the past century. The cause of the Wryneck's decline is not clear, though the loss of its insect food as a result of changes in farming practices, together with wetter summers during the period of decline, may have combined to send the species on a downward spiral. The Wryneck continues, however, to be fairly common and widespread in its main strongholds, Eastern Europe and Russia.

EURASIAN WRYNECK | *Jynx torquilla*

UNLIKE MOST OTHER WOODPECKERS, WRYNECKS ARE EQUALLY AT HOME
ON THE GROUND AS IN THE TREES

'It's like finding Elvis!' That was the verdict of one incredulous observer on the rediscovery of the Ivory-billed Woodpecker, one of North America's most endangered birds. The news broke in early 2005, when it was announced that the woodpecker had been sighted – and captured on video – in the swampy forests of Arkansas.

Last sighted in the USA during World War II, the finding of North America's largest woodpecker was a cause for celebration. If such an iconic bird could survive unseen for so long, surely there was hope for many other species presumed to be extinct.

For the nearby town of Brinkley, the news brought a welcome economic bonanza. Hordes of birders and curious tourists came in search of the bird, bringing much-needed revenue to a region blighted by poverty. Local storekeepers were quick to cash in, using images of the woodpecker to sell everything from burgers to haircuts. One local resident even wrote a song dedicated to the 'Lord God bird'.

Then, a year or so later, came the bombshell that shattered their hopes and dreams. David Sibley, creator of the eponymous *Sibley North American Bird Guide*, took a closer look at the video evidence of the bird. Although it undoubtedly showed a large, black-and-white woodpecker in flight, Sibley's expert eye made him realise that the smaller – and much more common – Pileated Woodpecker could not be ruled out. As a result, the claim that Ivory-bills had defied extinction could not be upheld. Since then the debate has raged back and forth, and the search goes on for this extraordinary bird.

The Ivory-billed Woodpecker was never common: breeding pairs require huge tracts of uncut forest, so it occurred in low densities across the southeastern USA, from Oklahoma to Florida. Once Europeans arrived and began cutting down the trees, the species was doomed. In 1935 an expedition to one of the species' last strongholds, the Singer Tract in Louisiana, filmed several birds; since then reports have been few and far between.

A separate, distinct race was also found on the island of Cuba. This population lingered on into the 1980s, though whether one or two birds still remain in the northwestern forests is open to debate.

What is tragic about the decline – and probable extinction – of the Ivory-billed Woodpecker is that the world's largest economy allowed one of its greatest natural treasures to decline to the point of no return. Then, having supposedly rediscovered the bird, more effort was put into exploiting its presence than into confirming whether or not the sighting was genuine. Maybe the comparison with Elvis Presley is not so far-fetched, after all.

An Ivory-billed Woodpecker photographed in Louisiana a few decades before the species was declared extinct

Campephilus principalis

IVORY-BILLED WOODPECKER

Gurney's Pitta is a flagship species for bird conservation, especially in the troubled region of southeast Asia, because of its inspiring comeback from the brink of extinction.

One of about 30 species in its family – an Old World group found in dense forest habitats from Africa, across southern Asia to Australasia – Gurney's Pitta is a plump, colourful passerine with a short tail and large, powerful bill.

Males sport a black head and blue crown, black underparts, a brown back and a bright yellow collar and flanks; females have a warm buffish-yellow crown, black mask, white throat, brown back and yellow underparts barred with black. Both are very striking – though, given their dense forest habitat, sightings are often restricted to brief glimpses in poor light conditions.

Within its forest habitat, Gurney's Pitta has quite specialised preferences: it tends to be found close to streams or gullies where it remains damp throughout the year. This enables it to find food more easily – insects, other invertebrates and small frogs, discovered by tossing the leaf-litter aside with flicks of its thick and powerful bill.

The species was originally named after the Victorian English ornithologist J. H. Gurney, by his friend, the doyen of Indian ornithology Allan Octavian Hume – though the actual specimen was in fact obtained by a collector employed by Hume, rather than by the great man himself. At the time it was considered to be fairly common, especially in southern Burma (Myanmar); but by the middle of the 20th century numbers had plummeted and the species was on the verge of extinction.

After 1952, when a specimen of Gurney's Pitta was collected in northern Thailand, it was not seen again for more than 30 years. Then, in 1986, ornithologists searching for this jewel of a bird rediscovered the species in one of Thailand's very few remaining areas of lowland rainforest. Despite conservation efforts, numbers continued to drop, from just over 40 pairs soon after its rediscovery to just 30 individuals by the turn of the millennium. Then came the welcome news that a small population – perhaps 100 pairs – had been discovered in a remote forest in Myanmar.

Two decades or so after its rediscovery, Gurney's Pitta is classed as 'Critically Endangered', and its fate is finely balanced, with forest clearance for timber and to make way for oil-palm plantations posing the greatest threat. Gurney's Pitta was the focus of the 2005 British Birdwatching Fair, when over £200,000 was raised to help save the species.

One of the most beautiful birds in the world – Gurney's Pitta is making a comeback from the brink of extinction

Pitta gurneyi | # GURNEY'S PITTA

STILL EXTREMELY RARE, WITH A POPULATION NUMBERING NOT MUCH MORE THAN ONE HUNDRED INDIVIDUALS, GURNEY'S PITTA IS ALSO ONE OF THE MOST BEAUTIFUL BIRDS IN THE WORLD

The four species of bellbird are members of that most diverse of all passerine bird families, the cotingas of Central and South America. Their claim to fame is that male bellbirds have what are probably the loudest calls in the bird world, peaking at up to 100 decibels – roughly the equivalent of a motor cycle or a pneumatic drill.

The name of the Bearded Bellbird is suitable and unsuitable in equal measure: suitable because the males do sport a tuft of feathers just beneath the lower mandible of the bill, which does look remarkably like a man's beard; unsuitable because the call sounds nothing like a bell (the name was originally attached to a different species, the White Bellbird).

The range of the Bearded Bellbird is highly discontinuous, with two distinctive races, one found in northern South America and Trinidad, the other in northeast Brazil, several thousand kilometres away. The northern race has a noticeably darker body – almost grey in appearance. Both share the same distinctive call, which sounds like an anvil being struck repeatedly and with determination with a hammer – giving rise to one local name, 'Anvil-bird'.

Once the male has attracted a female with his call, he changes his strategy, moving much lower down into the understorey of the forest and displaying to her alone. When she has accepted his entreaties and joined him on his perch, he gives a triumphant 'bock' call, and mating swiftly follows.

Bearded Bellbirds nest in trees, the female building a nest out of twigs, and laying a single egg, which she incubates entirely on her own. This leaves the male, who is polygamous, to seek out more females by uttering his famous song.

The male Bearded Bellbird has a contrasting plumage, with a silvery-white back, tail and underparts, black wings, and a chestnut-brown head with a black throat. The female is noticeably smaller, and lacks the beard; her plumage is mainly olive-green and yellow, with streaking along her flanks.

The chicks are covered by a thick coat of greyish-white down, unusual for a bird found in tropical climates. It has been suggested that this performs two quite distinct functions. Firstly, it keeps the chick warm when the female is absent from the nest; secondly, when the chick curls up, its appearance is supposed to mimic the hairy caterpillars avoided by most predators, as the hairs cause irritation to the skin. In contrast to the loud male, females and chicks are noticeably quiet at or near the nest to avoid drawing attention to themselves and attracting unwelcome predators.

The distinctive tuft of feathers beneath its bill has given the Bearded Bellbird its name

Procnias averano | # BEARDED BELLBIRD

THE DIET OF BOTH SEXES OF BEARDED BELLBIRD CONSISTS MAINLY OF THE FRUIT AND BERRIES OF A WIDE RANGE OF TROPICAL PLANTS, MOSTLY TAKEN ON THE WING, USING THE LARGE GAPE COMMON TO ALL FOUR SPECIES OF BELLBIRD

The national bird of Peru would have to be pretty special. After all, with more than 1,700 different species, the Peruvians are rather spoilt for choice. The Andean Cock-of-the-rock certainly fits the bill: not only is it one of the most beautiful and striking birds of this bird-rich continent, but it also boasts one of the world's most bizarre and fascinating courtship displays.

The Andean Cock-of-the-rock is one of two closely-related species (the other being the Guianan Cock-of-the-rock). Both are members of the cotinga family, a group of about 70 forest-dwelling species of the Neotropics. Its range extends in a long, narrow strip along the northern Andes, from Venezuela in the north, through Ecuador and Bolivia, to Peru.

Cotingas are very diverse in appearance: some very small, others large; some brightly coloured, others rather drab. The two cocks-of-the-rock are arguably the most distinctive species in the family: the males of both sport a bright orange-red plumage, and an extraordinary movable crest used in their courtship display. The Andean species is slightly larger than its cousin, with its dark wings and tail contrasting with the rest of the plumage.

Cocks-of-the-rock are another set of species that perform in a lek. Males gather in groups of up to 16 birds, then, like a morris-dancing team, form pairs and display to one another – in this case to impress the watching females. The aim is to get as close to the centre of the lek as possible as it is this position that attracts the most attention from females. The theory is that by mating with the male closest to the centre (i.e. the dominant male in the group), the female ensures that the very best genes are passed on to her offspring. Overall, the effect is highly impressive – at least to watching humans, if not to the females (hens-of-the-rock?!). Indeed, this courtship display is considered to rival the birds-of-paradise as one of the most spectacular in the avian world.

In common with other lekking species, once the birds have mated, the male plays no further part in nest-building or chick-rearing. Instead, the female is left to build the nest – not, as with most other tropical forest species, in a tree, but on an outcrop of rock. Here she constructs a cone-shaped structure from mud lined with vegetable fibre, attached to the face of the rock with saliva.

Their diet consists mainly of fruit, though adults will also eat insects. Lizards and frogs are an important constituent of the chicks' diet – being subdued by beating before they are fed to the young.

Not surprisingly for such a gaudy and noticeable bird, cocks-of-the-rock have played a central part in local culture throughout their range, though in most cases this has involved the birds themselves being sacrificed in order for a tribal chieftain to wear their feathers.

The striking plumage of the male Andean Cock-of-the-rock

Rupicola peruvianus

ANDEAN COCK-OF-THE-ROCK

In March 1983, rock legend Michael Jackson performed a new dance in public for the very first time. The 'moonwalk', a strange mixture of jerky movements unlike anything ever seen before, was an instant hit, being imitated by fans throughout the world. But how many of them were aware that Jackson might have been inspired by one of the world's most remarkable birds, the Red-capped Manakin?

The Red-capped Manakin has a relatively small range in Central and northern South America, from the extreme southeast of Mexico, through Costa Rica and Panama, to the western parts of Colombia and Ecuador. It is found in humid lowland forest and mature woodland, where it feeds mainly on insects (often taken in the air) and small fruits. The species is not classified as endangered, though as with all Neotropical forest birds, habitat loss through deforestation is a continual threat.

Confined to the tropical and equatorial regions of Central and South America, manakins are a group of compact, colourful birds, many of which are known for their complex and visually stunning courtship displays. But even amongst a family renowned for this aspect of their behaviour, the display of the Red-capped Manakin has to be seen to be believed.

The males first gather at their lek — a type of courtship that

The male Red-capped Manakin (left) 'doing the moonwalk'

is favoured by an eclectic range of species, but especially popular with members of the manakin family. At first, there appears to be little or no activity — at least until the first female arrives. At this point, the males begin to compete frantically with each other to attract her attention.

Each male will find a suitable perch, and then begin an extraordinary series of movements in order to impress on the female his suitability as a mate. First he simply hops back and forth, stretching his legs in order to reveal bright yellow feathering around his thighs. Then he flies off to another perch, his wings whirring to further impress his potential partner, only to turn around immediately and return to his original position.

Finally, he performs the famous 'backward-slide' display: lowering his head, lifting his tail, and apparently gliding effortlessly along the length of the branch, calling loudly and clicking his wings as he does so. In fact the manakin is moving his feet in very short steps, but so rapidly that to the human eye it appears as if he is sliding.

When several males gather together to woo a female, the resulting sound is like an outbreak of static electricity — making displaying birds much easier to find in the dense forest. Produced by the male's short wings, the aim of this bizarre sound is, in the words of one scientist, 'to blow the female's mind'.

RED-CAPPED MANAKIN | *Pipra mentalis*

ONE OBSERVER DESCRIBED THE COURTSHIP PERFORMANCE OF THE RED-CAPPED MANAKIN AS A CROSS BETWEEN MICHAEL JACKSON'S MOONWALK AND A TEENAGER ON AMPHETAMINES

Despite its name, the Noisy Scrub-bird is one of Australia's most elusive birds. Indeed, for more than 70 years, from the late 19th century to the early 1960s, it was assumed to have become extinct. Then, a tiny relict population was rediscovered on Mount Gardner, in a remote corner of southwestern Australia. With fewer than 100 individuals left alive, the Noisy Scrub-bird had overnight gained the unenviable status of Australia's rarest passerine.

Despite the remoteness of its location, the species faced considerable threats to its survival, including frequent bushfires and a proposed urban development at the foot of the mountain. Fortunately conservationists managed to safeguard the breeding area, and by the 1980s had begun a reintroduction programme, translocating surplus birds to other sites in the region. Today, the Noisy Scrub-bird population has risen to at least 2,000 individuals, on more than 600 breeding territories, at several sites. As a result, its conservation status has recently been downgraded from 'Endangered' to 'Vulnerable'.

For both Australian and visiting birders, the species remains one of the hardest to see. As its name suggests, it is normally located by its sound: the territorial song of the male is one of the loudest and most penetrating of any small bird. As with most songbirds, the times of greatest vocal activity

Australia's rarest passerine — the Noisy Scrub-bird

are dawn and dusk, though males will also sing through the night — and indeed during the middle of the day — especially in areas with a high density of territorial pairs.

In appearance, the Noisy Scrub-bird is rather less impressive. About the size of a small thrush, it has an elongated body, long tail and horizontal posture typical of a species that spends most of its time foraging on the ground. The plumage is basically rufous-brown, with whitish underparts; males also have a dark throat-patch. The wings are very short, as befits this sedentary species.

Since they were first discovered in the mid-19th century, the two species of scrub-birds (the other being the smaller Rufous Scrub-bird, found in eastern Australia) have posed a puzzle for taxonomists. Most theories suggest that their closest relatives are another bizarre Australian passerine family, the lyrebirds — though, unlike that group, they do not have such showy courtship displays or a power of mimicry.

Like many Australian songbirds, however, they do build a fairly elaborate nest, with a domed entrance, lined with decaying wood which forms a papier-mâché-like base. Another remarkable feature is that their single egg takes more than five weeks to hatch — one of the longest incubation periods of any of the world's 6,000 or so species of songbird.

NOISY SCRUB-BIRD | *Atrichornis clamosus*

ONCE HEARD, THE SONG OF THE NOISY SCRUB-BIRD IS UNLIKELY TO BE FORGOTTEN: IT STARTS WITH A SERIES OF LOUD, FORCEFUL NOTES, RISING IN PITCH, FOLLOWED BY A TORRENT OF BELL-LIKE SOUNDS, OFTEN ENDING AS ABRUPTLY AS IT BEGAN

A bird that looks like a pheasant, has one of the world's most amazing courtship displays, and possesses skills of mimicry to rival any bird on earth, was always going to puzzle scientists. Since European explorers originally discovered them in eastern Australia in the late 18th century, lyrebirds have certainly managed to do that.

When the earliest specimens were sent back to England for examination, lyrebirds were at first considered to be related to gamebirds, and later presumed to be an Australian form of bird-of-paradise. It took more than 40 years before the birds' true affinity – part of the world's largest order of birds, the passerines – was finally understood. Today, DNA studies have confirmed that the lyrebirds are, along with another peculiar family of Australian passerines, the scrub-birds, essentially in a group of their own.

The Superb Lyrebird is by far the best-known of the two species in the family. Its close relative, Albert's Lyrebird, is now quite rare, with only about 10,000 individuals living in a tiny area of eastern Australia, where they are potentially threatened with extinction. The much commoner Superb Lyrebird is also an eastern Australian endemic, found in a fairly narrow coastal strip of moist temperate or subtropical rainforest from southeast Queensland through eastern New South Wales to eastern Victoria. There is also a small introduced population on the island of Tasmania.

The bird is named after its extraordinary tail, which, when held aloft in courtship, reminded its discoverers of the stringed instrument popular in Ancient Greece. The tail itself is made up of 16 highly modified feathers, of which the outermost pair forms the elongated lyre-shaped plumes.

In contrast to this spectacular appendage, the wings are short and rounded, and rarely used. Instead lyrebirds mainly move on foot, using their long, powerful legs and feet to run around their forest territory. However, to avoid predators they do roost in trees, at heights of up to 45 metres – involving frantic flapping and leaping from branch to branch in order to get aloft.

The male Superb Lyrebird is justly famous for his extraordinary courtship display, in which he first builds a large number of display mounds, using his powerful claws to scrape away the leaf litter and move the earth into a pile. Then he fans out his tail into its fully open position, and prances around in order to attract the female to mate with him.

As he does so, he makes a series of bizarre vocalisations, incorporating a wide range of natural and non-natural sounds – a phenomenon captured for posterity on David Attenborough's television series *The Life of Birds*.

It is the extraordinary lyre-shaped plumes that give the Superb Lyrebird its name

Menura novaehollandiae | # SUPERB LYREBIRD

LYREBIRDS HAVE BEEN KNOWN TO IMITATE CHAIN-SAWS, DINGOES, AND EVEN THE SHUTTER AND MOTOR-DRIVE OF AN SLR CAMERA

It is a reflection of our emotional link with birdsong that the two birds most celebrated in English poetry are both 'little brown jobs' – the nightingale and the Skylark. Despite the drabness of their plumage, both take their place at the very top of avian inspirations for poets.

In the case of the Eurasian Skylark, the tradition goes back to the very beginnings of modern English: the 15th-century Scottish poet William Dunbar wrote that 'the skyes rang for the shouting of larks' – a vivid description of the bird's song-flight.

Later, 19th-century poets including Clare and Shelley also wrote of the bird. Clare described it, with characteristic bluntness, as 'a dust-spot in the sunny skies', while Shelley created an altogether grander vision, in what is a candidate for the best-known couplet in English poetry:

Hail to thee, Blithe Spirit!
Bird thou never wert.

The bird that inspired this praise is one of almost a hundred species of lark whose stronghold is the dry deserts and grasslands of Africa and Asia.

Apart from the Horned (Shore) Lark, which has colonised North America, the Skylark has the widest range of all its family. From Ireland and Portugal in the west, to

This 'little brown job' is an extraordinary songbird

Japan and Sakhalin in the east, it breeds across the whole of temperate Europe and Asia. It is able to do so because unlike many of its relatives, which are confined to mainly dry, desert-type habitats, it has evolved a preference for a whole range of open ground, from farmland to heathland, and moorland to coastal marshes.

It is this catholic choice of breeding sites that made the Skylark Britain's most widespread bird during the first Atlas survey, in the late 1960s and early 1970s. Since then, its inability to adapt to farmland has proved to be its Achilles' heel. Although well suited to traditional farming methods, it suffered greatly from the post-war agricultural revolution that created 'improved' grassland unsuitable for larks to nest.

The Skylark is best known for its extraordinary song-flight, in which the male lark appears to hang in the air for hours on end, singing as if his life depended on it. Which in a way it does: a recent theory suggests that by revealing himself to potential aerial predators such as falcons, the lark is taking a major gamble. Having exposed himself to potential attack, his only option is to sing even louder and longer than his rivals, to show that if he were attacked he would easily be able to escape. If true, this is a remarkable example of the 'handicap principle', in which to show how fit it is, a prey animal deliberately advertises its presence to predators.

EURASIAN SKYLARK | *Alauda arvensis*

UNTIL THE 17TH CENTURY THE EURASIAN SKYLARK WAS KNOWN SIMPLY AS THE 'LARK'. THE NAME WE NOW KNOW AND LOVE WAS CREATED BY THE GREAT ENGLISH NATURALIST JOHN RAY

As they prepare for migration, in late summer and early autumn, Barn Swallows can often be seen flying low over the surface of a lake or pond, skimming the water with their bills to obtain much-needed refreshment. It was after observing this that the father of modern natural history, the 18th-century clergyman Gilbert White, made one of his few major errors, suggesting that rather than migrating south for the winter, Swallows in fact hibernated somewhere beneath the water's surface.

The truth that Gilbert White found so difficult to believe is hardly less incredible. After leaving their breeding areas in the temperate regions of Europe, Asia or North America, Swallows fly up to 10,000 km to reach their wintering grounds in South America, southern Africa, Asia and Australia. Not only that, but juvenile birds do the journey only a few weeks after leaving the nest, with no guidance from their parents – and return to the area where they were born the following spring!

No wonder that the Swallow rivals the Cuckoo as the definitive sign that winter is over, spring is here, and summer is on the way. Swallows appear throughout European folklore, while the bird is also mentioned in Ancient Greek myths and legends, and in the Old Testament as well as the Koran.

Swallows complete a long migration to their wintering grounds and are a sign of the arrival of spring

Unlike most passerines, Swallows are day-flying migrants, keeping fairly low to the ground in order to stop and feed regularly on tiny flying insects. This does leave them vulnerable to predators such as falcons, though their speed and agility usually allows them to escape. Their long wings and forked tail are an asset not only on their travels: they also allow Swallows to pursue their prey with acrobatic twists and turns.

Long associated with farms and especially farmyards, Swallows appear to have suffered less than many farmland birds from the agricultural revolution that swept North America and Europe in the decades following World War II. Nevertheless the widespread loss of livestock on modern farms – and the resulting lack of insect food – has led to some declines.

The name 'swallow', originally given to this species but now also used for dozens more, is one of the oldest of all bird names, as can be deduced from the fact that it occurs with minor variations in many Germanic and Scandinavian languages. It derives from a word meaning 'cleft stick', which refers to the bird's long tail. Today the species is known officially as Barn Swallow to distinguish it from its relatives; now-defunct English names include Chimney Swallow and, confusingly (given the existence of the House Martin), House Swallow.

BARN SWALLOW | *Hirundo rustica*

'ONE SWALLOW DOESN'T MAKE A SUMMER' MAY BE TRUE, BUT THE SIGHT OF A DOZEN BIRDS HAWKING FOR INSECTS ON A WARM APRIL DAY BRINGS JOY TO THE HEARTS OF PEOPLE THROUGHOUT THE NORTHERN HEMISPHERE

Supermarket car parks are not normally known for their attraction for birds, with one notable exception. From time to time, as Christmas shoppers in Britain load up their trolleys in preparation for the festive season ahead, there come reports of flocks of strange and exotic birds appearing in these unlikely venues.

They are Bohemian Waxwings, attracted by the bushes laden with berries – bushes planted to lend a spuriously natural air to the concrete and brickwork of their surroundings. They do not come every winter and their appearances are irregular and unpredictable. But when they do turn up they are guaranteed a warm reception from anyone fortunate enough to see these beautiful birds.

The Bohemian Waxwing is the largest and by far the most widespread of the three species in its family, breeding across a wide swathe of the nortern hemisphere from Scandinavia east across Siberia, as well as in Canada and the northern United States. One close relative, the Cedar Waxwing, is confined to North America, where its range overlaps extensively with this species. The other, the Japanese Waxwing, has a much more restricted distribution, breeding in southeast Russia and northeast China, and wintering in eastern China, Korea and Japan. All three species are plump, medium-sized passerines with subtle brown shades of plumage, red and yellow markings, a black throat and a silky crest.

Waxwings are named after the peculiar wax-like tips to the feathers on the secondary feathers of the wing, a unique family trait. The name 'waxwing' is in fact a relatively recent one, coined less than 200 years ago. Because of its wanderings, the name Bohemian has been attached to the species for far longer, from at least the middle of the 16th century.

All three waxwings are known for their nomadic wanderings – properly known as irruptions – however. These annual movements are governed by various factors to do with food supply and breeding success: irruption years are likely to occur after a successful breeding season and a poor berry crop, so that too many birds are chasing too little food. In one celebrated 'Waxwing year', 1965/66, flocks numbering thousands of birds reached Germany and Britain, while smaller groups ventured as far afield as the Mediterranean.

Having arrived in a particular area in autumn, Waxwings will methodically strip bushes of their fruit before moving on to another food supply, either locally or some distance away. They remain on their wintering areas until the following spring, when they head back north to breed.

A Bohemian Waxwing feeding on rowan berries in Worcestershire, England

Bombycilla garrulus | # BOHEMIAN WAXWING

ODDLY FOR SUCH A SILENT SPECIES, THE BOHEMIAN WAXWING WAS KNOWN AS THE 'BOHEMIAN CHATTERER' AND 'WAXEN CHATTERER' UNTIL THE CURRENT NAME GAINED WIDESPREAD ACCEPTANCE FROM THE EARLY 19TH CENTURY

Discovered and named by a descendant of the Emperor Napoleon, this southwest Asian endemic looks like a cross between a bulbul and a shrike, but is most closely related to the waxwings. Nevertheless, it is sufficiently different from the members of that group to merit being placed on its own in a single-species family.

The breeding range of the Hypocolius covers a fairly restricted area, from eastern Iraq through Iran and Turkmenistan to western Afghanistan, placing it in one of the most turbulent and politically unstable regions in the world. Indeed, a large proportion of the world population breeds in the marshes of southern Iraq, an area in almost constant turmoil.

Outside the breeding season, the Hypocolius moves southwards, its winter range extending as far as Saudi Arabia, western India and the Gulf states of the United Arab Emirates and Oman, bringing it within the sights of western European birders eager to see this peculiar but strangely attractive bird.

The Hypocolius is a distinctive species, and given good views is easily identified. It is about the size of a thrush, but much slimmer and with a long tail. Males are greyer than the brownish females, and sport a prominent black patch across the face, as well as a black tip to the tail.

It has been suggested that the species has actually benefited from living alongside people: formerly dry and inhospitable habitats have been irrigated and planted with fruit trees, providing a ready supply of food and water in a hostile environment. However, this can have its downside: large numbers of birds roosting in Bahrain suffered the wholesale destruction of their winter roost site when it was bulldozed for development.

In their breeding areas, Hypocoliuses seek out areas of low scrub, often in river valleys where they can get easy access to water for drinking and bathing. They have a particular preference for a low, scrubby bush named *Salvatora persica*, known colloquially as the 'toothbrush tree', because its fibrous twigs have long been used by Muslims to clean their teeth, especially before prayer. The requirements of the Hypocolius are rather simpler: they feed voraciously on the fruits of this famous plant. Like its close relatives the waxwings, the Hypocolius is primarily a fruit-eater, but when the opportunity presents itself it will feed on flying insects, which it catches with acrobatic aerial sallies on its long, slender wings.

Despite its relatively small world range, the Hypocolius is numerous and adaptable enough not to be considered globally threatened. However, given the instability and warfare throughout many of its breeding areas, conservationists continue to keep a watch on this unusual and attractive bird.

The Hypocolius, a southwest Asian speciality

Hypocolius ampelinus | # HYPOCOLIUS

HYPOCOLIUSES ARE GREGARIOUS AND SOCIABLE BIRDS, AND HAVE ADAPTED WELL TO THE PRESENCE OF HUMAN BEINGS, OFTEN FEEDING IN PARKS AND GARDENS

There are more than 80 species of wren, found throughout the Americas from Alaska in the north to Patagonia in the south. They are highly adaptable birds, found in habitats ranging from gardens to deserts, and from forests to coastal marshes. However, one species from this diverse family has managed an even more remarkable feat of colonisation: having crossed the Bering Strait from North America into Asia, the Winter (or Northern) Wren moved on into three continents, becoming the most widespread wren in the world.

Today, the Wren, as this species is usually known, can be found from Iceland and Morocco in the west to Kamchatka and Japan in the east, as well as across much of North America. What is even more remarkable is that this little brown bird has adapted to a wider range of habitats than virtually any other species.

In the course of this remarkable colonisation, the Wren has evolved into at least forty different races or subspecies. The nominate race – named in 1758 by the father of taxonomy, the Swedish botanist Linnaeus – is found across much of mainland Europe, from Scandinavia to the Urals, and from the Iberian Peninsula to Greece.

Other races include some confined to a single island or island group. These include the Fair Isle Wren, the Shetland Wren and, most famously, the St Kilda Wren – a larger, darker version of this familiar bird, with a noticeably louder song..

That is not to say that the other races of the Wren are quiet! Indeed, it is hard to recall another species whose volume-to-size ratio is quite so impressive: how can a bird weighing just 10 grams produce such a sound? The sight of a male Wren in full song – compared by one observer to an operatic diva reaching the climax of her performance – is truly remarkable.

His energy is not confined to his singing. Male Wrens are famed for building as many as eight different 'cock's nests', each of which is carefully examined by the female until she is satisfied that she has found the best one. Only then will she consent to mate and form a pair bond. The female will lay up to nine tiny eggs, which if food supplies are available will allow the parents to raise an impressively large brood.

Wrens are, however, highly susceptible to cold winters, perishing in vast numbers during prolonged freezes such as the winter of 1962/63, which brought Britain to a standstill for over three months. However, the recent run of mild winters, almost certainly a result of global climate change, has allowed many more young Wrens to survive the winter. As a result, the species has gone from being Britain and Ireland's fifth-commonest bird to their most numerous, with as many as ten million breeding pairs.

A Winter Wren in full song – a sight to behold

Troglodytes troglodytes | # WINTER WREN

WRENS CAN BE FOUND ON REMOTE OFFSHORE ISLANDS, IN SUBURBAN GARDENS, MIXED WOODLAND, MOORLAND SCRUB, AND ON THE SLOPES OF THE HIMALAYAS

Made famous throughout the world by the title of Harper Lee's 1960 novel *To Kill a Mockingbird* (and the subsequent film starring Gregory Peck), this brash and distinctive-sounding species is widespread in the towns and suburbs of North America.

Like the Old World thrushes, to which the family is distantly related, mockingbirds have long been celebrated for their extraordinary vocal powers. As well as a tuneful and memorable song, they also have the ability to mimic other birds, together with various non-avian sounds, including frogs and mechanical devices – hence this species' scientific name.

The repertoire of the Northern Mockingbird comprises at least 150 distinctive tunes – an impressive number, but one that pales into insignificance compared with that of its close relative the Brown Thrasher. This latter species has been known to sing up to 2,000 different songs, making it the world's champion songster. Nevertheless, mockingbirds are quick learners, and will continue to add sounds to their repertoire throughout their lives.

When not singing, mockingbirds spend much of the time hopping around on the ground at the base of bushes and scrub, or across well-mown lawns. They are searching for a variety of food items including beetles, ants and worms, though they will also feed on plant matter such as berries.

A Northern Mockingbird defends its holly bush

Mockingbirds have benefited from the human conquest of North America, as gardens are highly productive sources of food and nesting places. In return, they act as a natural pest controller for gardeners, and so are generally welcomed. But mockingbirds are not loved by everyone: as well-known nocturnal songsters, they are unpopular with insomniacs. As one of the continent's most widespread birds, the species also has an instant recognition factor. The Northern Mockingbird has been adopted as the state bird for Arkansas, Florida, Mississippi, Tennessee and Texas – only the Northern Cardinal and Western Meadowlark are more popular.

When nesting, male mockingbirds are fiercely territorial. They have been known to mob passers-by, and can even recognise individual human beings and single them out for attack. It is tempting to think this is in revenge for the cagebird trade of the early 20th century, which temporarily threatened to wipe out mockingbird populations in some parts of North America.

While the Northern Mockingbird is common and widespread, ranging from southwest Canada to the south of Mexico, some of its relatives are highly localised and endangered. The Galápagos Archipelago, for example, is home to no fewer than four distinct mockingbird species, three of which are confined to just one or two islands.

NORTHERN MOCKINGBIRD | *Mimus polyglottos*

LIKE THRUSHES, MOCKINGBIRDS ARE KNOWN TO DEFEND WINTER TERRITORIES WITH BERRY BUSHES, AGGRESSIVELY SEEING OFF ANY COMPETITORS AND MAKING SURE THEY GET THE BEST FRUIT FOR THEMSELVES

When the earliest English settlers crossed the Atlantic to make a new home in the wilds of North America, one can imagine their fear and trepidation about the dangers present in this unexplored and unknown country. So it is hardly surprising that when they came across a bird sporting a red breast, these homesick voyagers named it after their favourite bird back home. Thus it was that a large thrush of the genus *Turdus* – more closely related to the European Blackbird than to its namesake – still bears the name of American Robin.

Ever since that first encounter, the relationship between these birds and human beings has always been close. Originally a bird of mature forests, it now breeds in any kind of woodland, as well as on farms and homesteads, and in parks and gardens.

Although it breeds throughout North America, it is especially widespread in the eastern states, and is the state bird for Connecticut, Michigan and Wisconsin. In the latest US Great Backyard Bird Count it did not quite make the top ten of most reported birds, though in numbers alone it ranked seventh, with almost 300,000 individuals reported.

One of the reasons for the species' success is that it is able to switch its diet from season to season, depending on the availability of food. So in spring and early summer American Robins feed almost exclusively on

An American Robin – the most widespread thrush in North America

invertebrates – mainly caterpillars and beetles – whereas in autumn and winter they mainly eat fruit and berries. When feeding their young the adults are admirably unselfish, eating the smaller prey items while giving the larger ones to their chicks.

The American Robin remains North America's commonest and most widespread species of thrush, though as with all species that regularly feed on farmland it remains vulnerable to localised deaths from agricultural pesticides, such as a crop-spraying incident in Florida in 1972 that killed more than 10,000 birds.

Despite their scientific name, American Robins are only fully migratory in the northern parts of their range, such as Canada and the northern states of the USA. However, their habit of migrating during the day in vast, noisy flocks means that they are a familiar sight at watchpoints such as Cape May in New Jersey. Occasionally birds go adrift, even reaching western Europe on occasion. Having flown all the way to Britain, one unfortunate individual was taken by a Sparrowhawk, to the dismay of watching birders.

Another American Robin also turned up in London – though this time in fiction rather than reality. In the 1964 Disney film *Mary Poppins*, two birds seen building a nest are both – incorrectly of course – American Robins rather than the European variety.

AMERICAN ROBIN | *Turdus migratorius*

TODAY, THE AMERICAN ROBIN IS ARGUABLY AMERICA'S MOST FAMILIAR AND WELL-LOVED BIRD, HAVING TAKEN FULL ADVANTAGE OF ITS ABILITY TO LIVE ALONGSIDE PEOPLE

There are many small, brownish birds in the world, so many that birders have invented a rather disparaging name for them: 'little brown jobs' or LBJs. Most are unmemorable at best, instantly forgettable at worst, and are about as likely to feature in a book of the world's one hundred most remarkable birds as they are to fly to the moon.

Yet one member of the family *Muscicapidae*, saddled with the scientific name *Luscinia megarhynchos*, has achieved virtually universal fame, even in cultures many thousands of kilometres from its native home. The name of this unlikely celebrity? The Nightingale.

The Common Nightingale has been celebrated by poets, playwrights and composers since the dawn of civilisation. Pliny wrote about it, as did Aristotle. The species is featured in one of the earliest poems in modern English, the 13th-century 'The Owl and the Nightingale'. Shakespeare wrote about the bird, as, famously, did Keats and T. S. Eliot. It has inspired composers from Beethoven to Tchaikovsky, and was the subject of one of the 20th century's most popular songs, 'A Nightingale Sang in Berkeley Square'.

The reason for the Common (or Rufous) Nightingale's continued and worldwide fame is, of course, its extraordinary song. It is not, perhaps, the most

One of the most celebrated of songbirds – the Common Nightingale

beautiful or tuneful in the world, nor even the loudest – but certainly the most remarkable. Its key is its unpredictability: like a jazz musician, the male Nightingale impro-vises, using a 'songbook' of anything up to 300 different tunes, so that the listener can never be quite sure what is coming next.

With such a unique song, you might imagine that it would be impossible to confuse the Common Nightingale with any other bird. Nevertheless, there are many examples of lesser songsters being mistaken for the real thing. The Blackcap was once given the folk name of 'March Nightingale' because its fluty song, delivered several months earlier than that of the Nightingale, would confuse unwary listeners.

Poets have used the Nightingale and its song to symbolise many human emotions, generally centred on the twin themes of love and melancholy. During World War I the latter theme predominated, with soldiers in the trenches finding at least some consolation in the sad beauty of the Nightingale's song. As one front-line soldier, J.C. Faraday, wrote:

You will have a terrific roaring noise of artillery in the dead of night; then great quietness, when lo! and behold, out come the nightingales, right about the guns … and beautiful thoughts come along to relieve you from the devilment of war and the men who cause it.

COMMON NIGHTINGALE | *Luscinia megarhynchos*

THE PAUSES AND BREAKS IN THE NIGHTINGALE'S SONG ARE JUST AS IMPORTANT AS
THE ACTUAL NOTES, HELPING TO CREATE A UNIQUE AURAL EXPERIENCE

On 10 April 1773, a pair of unusual birds was 'obtained' (a euphemism for shot) on Bexley Heath, near the town of Dartford in Kent. The male was rather brighter than the female, but both sported dark, slate-grey upperparts and rich, burgundy-coloured underparts, together with a distinctively long, cocked tail.

The finder was unable to identify the specimens, so he sent them to ornithologist Thomas Pennant for examination. Realising that they were a species new to science, Pennant named them after the nearby town – since when this attractive little bird has been known as the Dartford Warbler.

The Dartford Warbler is one of a subgroup of small, short-winged warblers found around the Mediterranean. Despite its obvious similarity with Marmora's and Balearic Warblers, whose range it overlaps, its closest relative is now considered to be a little-known North African endemic species, Tristram's Warbler.

The westerly distribution of these species, close to the maritime influence of the Atlantic Ocean, is what sets them apart from most other *Sylvia* warblers, which either have an extensive range across much of Europe and Asia (e.g. Whitethroat, Blackcap) or are found in the more arid areas of southwest Asia and the Middle East (e.g. Desert and Arabian Warblers). Also in contrast to most European warblers, the Dartford Warbler is only a short-distance migrant: indeed across much of its range it is resident, staying put on or near its breeding areas throughout the year.

The Dartford Warbler is often considered a typical bird of lowland heath, and in Britain that is largely true: it once earned the folk name of 'Furze Wren' because of its cocked tail and predilection for nesting in or near gorse bushes. However, in the species' heartlands, such as Spain and western France, it shows a much more catholic choice of habitat, including open pine woodland and the typical Mediterranean *maquis* – low, dense evergreen shrubland similar to the North American *chaparral*.

In the northern part of its range the Dartford Warbler is highly susceptible to cold winters: the famous 'Big Freeze' of 1962/63 reduced the British population to a mere dozen pairs. However, after a long run of very mild winters the species has made a dramatic comeback, extending its range northwards. But although over 2,000 pairs now breed in Britain, this pales into insignificance compared with more than two million pairs in Spain. Perhaps it should be renamed Alicante Warbler.

The Dartford Warbler's folk name of 'Furze Wren' is very apt

Sylvia undata | # DARTFORD WARBLER

EVEN BY THE PAROCHIAL STANDARDS OF BRITISH ORNITHOLOGY, DARTFORD WARBLER IS A SINGULARLY INAPPROPRIATE NAME

The jungles of west and central Africa are home to some peculiar creatures, but few are as bizarre as the two species of picathartes – also known as 'rockfowl'. The White-necked Picathartes is found from Guinea through Sierra Leone and Liberia to the Ivory Coast, while the range of the Grey-necked Picathartes runs from southeast Nigeria through Cameroon and Gabon to Equatorial Guinea.

Both species are classified as 'Vulnerable', with population estimates for each ranging from just 2,500 to 10,000 individuals. Recent discoveries of nest sites in Gabon and Nigeria give some hope that the numbers of the Grey-necked Picathartes may have been underestimated in the past. However, like so many African forest species, it is very vulnerable to disturbance and habitat destruction.

In appearance, the Grey-necked Picathartes is very different from typical songbirds: more like a lanky crow, with a powerful bill, long tail and legs, on which it hops around its rocky habitat. Its most unusual feature, however, is its unfeathered head, with bold, brightly coloured patterns of lilac, carmine and black used in courtship displays. The rest of the body is grey on the upperparts and white on the underparts, shading to yellow on the belly.

Both species of Picathartes often breed colonially, building an unusual nest out of mud, attached to the roof of a cave or an overhanging rock on a cliff, where they lay two eggs. The nest sites are chosen very carefully, as the birds need an overhanging rock above to protect them from rain, and a sheer cliff below to prevent predators reaching the nest. They rarely fly very far, and mostly move around their rocky habitat on foot, with characteristically jerky hops.

Picathartes feed mainly on invertebrates, and like the antbirds of South America will often follow columns of army ants as they march through the forest, feeding on the insects, frogs and lizards disturbed as the troops of ants pass by.

One British bird artist spent three months searching for Grey-necked Picathartes on Mount Kupe in the heart of Cameroon. Having almost given up hope, he heard a hissing sound behind him. Fearing that he was about to be struck by a viper, he turned in trepidation, to see a Picathartes a mere two metres away, staring right at him. As he recalls, 'For a few minutes I faced him in awe before, like Zebedee, he sprang away.'

A Grey-necked Picathartes on its
nest within a cave

Picathartes
oreas

GREY-NECKED PICATHARTES

This stunningly beautiful bird – a fleeting vision of pink, grey and black – has an almost mythological status amongst birders. Apart from its sheer beauty, this may be because the Wallcreeper rarely ventures away from its remote mountain homes, though, from time to time, wandering individuals have taken up residence in some bizarre places.

As a breeding bird, the Wallcreeper has a very fragmented range due to its preference for high altitudes. It lives in mountainous regions from western and southern Europe, through the Middle East and across central Asia, usually in moist areas where small insects and spiders – its main diet – can be found. It obtains prey by probing into cracks and crevices with its long, narrow, decurved bill, and occasionally by flycatching.

Wallcreepers nest in cavities on the sides of rocks, in places chosen to be as inaccessible as possible to mammalian predators such as stoats and martens. They are generally sedentary, though some birds do head down to lower altitudes in autumn, often spending the winter in stone quarries, whose steep sides resemble their natural habitat.

Despite its remote haunts, however, the beauty of this bird often captures the imagination; as a result the Wallcreeper has featured on stamps from at least a dozen countries, including Andorra, Monaco and the former Yugoslavia. The Chinese name for the Wallcreeper is rather more poetic than the English one, translating as 'rock flower'. This image makes sense when the bird takes to the wing, revealing a deep pink wing-pattern, edged with black and tipped with white – a dramatic contrast with the steel-grey head and body. This colour is vital as a means of making contact with other birds, as the bird is generally rather quiet.

The rounded wings have evolved to allow the Wallcreeper to manoeuvre more easily when ascending or descending steep rock faces. When on the ground, the bird moves in jerky hops, recalling its close relatives the rock nuthatches.

A favourite wintering site is a Bavarian castle built by Emperor Ludwig II of Bavaria – a location used for the 1968 children's film *Chitty Chitty Bang Bang*. Some venture even further afield: in the 1970s, one spent successive winters at Cheddar Gorge in southwest England, while another could be seen at the University of Amsterdam. Here, it passed the time clinging to the surface of a wall as students passed beneath, often oblivious to the presence of this beautiful bird.

The vivid plumage of the Wallcreeper on an inaccessible rock face

WALLCREEPER | *Tichodroma muraria*

AS ONE OF EUROPE'S MOST BEAUTIFUL BIRDS, A WANDERING WALLCREEPER ALWAYS ATTRACTS LARGE CROWDS

The first sign that a party of Long-tailed Tits is about to appear is a chorus of soft, high-pitched calls, followed by the arrival of what one observer has described as 'flying lollipops' shooting along the top of a hedge.

Often, they come so close you could reach out and touch them: not because they are fearless, but simply because they are so concerned with finding their tiny insect food they don't have time to worry about anything in their path. Then, as suddenly as they appeared, they are gone, moving on in search of new places to feed.

In winter, parties of Long-tailed Tits are a familiar sight throughout the temperate regions of Europe and Asia, as far east as China. Of all the passerines in the region this species has the longest tail in relation to its body, making up well over half its total length.

At just 7–10 g in weight the Long-tailed Tit is also one of the lightest birds in the region, as a result of which it is especially vulnerable to hard winters. Flocking – a strategy by which more birds are likely to find more food – is therefore essential.

Even so, when winter temperatures plummet for long periods, as in the winters of 1916/17, 1946/47 and 1962/63 in Britain and northwestern Europe, the species is particularly hard hit, with a mortality rate of 80 per cent or more. Fortunately, like other small passerines

The Long-tailed Tit resembles a ball of fluff with a tail!

such as the Wren and Goldcrest, Long-tailed Tits are prolific breeders, and usually manage to replenish their population levels within a few years.

Despite their name, Long-tailed Tits are only distantly related to the true tits. They are the only European and Asian representative of a group of eight species, most of the rest of which – including the Bushtit – are found in North and Central America. Like other members of their family, they are known for their sociable behaviour, especially when breeding, when the parent birds are often helped out by other family members – quite an unusual practice in the bird world. After the chicks fledge, Long-tailed Tits stay in family parties throughout the autumn and winter.

It is for its nest that this charming little bird really qualifies as remarkable. A ball-shaped structure, it is carefully constructed using a mixture of moss, wool, silk from spider's webs and lichens. But the really amazing ingredient is feathers – as many as 2,300 in a single nest, each gathered by the parent birds, and woven into the construction to create a little miracle of nest-building.

Although the Long-tailed Tit has many folk names related to its appearance – including 'Ragamuffin' and 'Mufflin' – the majority of country names refer to its nest. These include 'Feather Poke', 'Bush Oven', and my personal favourite, 'Bumbarrel' – which could just as easily derive from the appearance of the bird itself.

LONG-TAILED TIT | *Aegithalos caudatus*

THIS CHARMING LITTLE BIRD IS WELL KNOWN FOR ITS GREGARIOUS, SOCIAL HABITS

The 30 or so species of shrike are amongst the most charismatic and fascinating of all the world's song-birds. Their striking plumage, custom of sitting in full view on top of a bush or tree, and predatory feeding habits, all give them the air of a miniature raptor rather than a passerine.

The Red-backed Shrike is one of the best-known members of its family. Easily the commonest Western Palaearctic shrike, it breeds across a wide swathe of Europe and western Asia, though in recent years it has suffered a major contraction of its range in the northwest, becoming extinct as a breeding bird in Britain. It is a long-distance migrant, heading thousands of kilometres south in autumn to spend the winter in Africa, almost entirely south of the equator.

Shrikes hunt using a 'sit-and-wait' technique: sitting quiet and still on a favourite perch until they spot a suitable victim, which they will then pounce on and grab, bringing it back to the perch. Before the species began its inexorable decline in Britain, the Red-backed Shrike was common and familiar enough to acquire the folk name of 'Butcher-bird'. This arose from its grisly habit of impaling prey items – such as beetles, frogs and baby birds – on the twigs of bushes such as hawthorn and black-thorn. This behaviour is more frequent on the northern and western edges of its range, where prolonged wet weather may make it difficult to catch prey; should this happen the shrike has a handy 'larder' on which to feed itself and its young until the weather improves.

Despite their brutal reputation – including the nicknames 'murdering pie' and 'nine killer' – shrikes frequently become the victim themselves, by having their nest parasitised by Cuckoos.

After breeding, Red-backed Shrikes head around the eastern side of the Mediterranean, passing through the Middle East on their way south, in a journey which can take more than three months. They share their wintering grounds with several other members of their family, including Lesser Grey and Isabelline Shrikes.

The African savannah also plays host to several resident species of shrike, as well as a whole range of related species such as boubous, tchagras and bush-shrikes, many of which have a similar appearance and habits. Despite this apparent competition, how-ever, there is plenty of food to go around.

In spring, the Red-backed Shrikes' return journey takes about half the time of the autumn migration, the birds leaving their winter quarters in early March and arriving back on their breeding grounds by the end of April or early May, to resume their lethal behaviour.

'Butcher-bird', 'murdering pie', 'nine killer' – all folk names of the Red-backed Shrike

Lanius collurio | # RED-BACKED SHRIKE

RED-BACKED SHRIKES HAVE ATTRACTED THEIR FAIR SHARE OF FOLKLORE, INCLUDING THE BELIEF THAT A SHRIKE KILLS NINE TIMES BEFORE IT BEGINS TO FEED

In 1996, a television film crew led by the doyen of wildlife presenters, David Attenborough, travelled through the rainforests of New Guinea in order to capture one of the world's unique bird spectacles on film for the first time. They experienced many technical problems but, once these had been overcome, they eventually succeeded and the resulting programme, *Attenborough in Paradise*, showed the extraordinary courtship display of Wilson's Bird-of-paradise.

The size of a starling, this Indonesian endemic is one of the most beautiful birds in the world. The male is mainly red and black, with a yellow patch on its neck, bright blue head and feet, and two huge, curved tail-feathers in a fetching shade of violet. As with other members of this family, the female is much less striking than the male: basically brown with a blue crown.

The bird was named not after the famous Scottish ornithologist Alexander Wilson, but for Edward Wilson, who had purchased the unidentified specimen from a trader. The first man to describe the species, Charles Lucien Bonaparte, gave it the controversial scientific name *respublica*. He did so to commemorate his fiercely republican beliefs – as the nephew of the celebrated Napoleon Bonaparte, he was used to controversy. The breeding grounds of Wilson's Bird-of-paradise – the islands of Waigeo

and Batanta, off the west coast of New Guinea – were not discovered until more than a decade later.

New Guinea is home to the vast majority of the 40 or so species of birds-of-paradise. Perhaps because of the remoteness of their forest homes, none of the birds-of-paradise is yet classified as 'Endangered', but this may well change in the coming decades. As with so many tropical species, habitat loss, combined with a limited range and the continued threat from exploitation by humans, means we must continue to be vigilant.

Birds-of-paradise have evolved a number of distinctive plumage features. Males have ornate feathering, including plumes, 'wires' (specially developed feathers protruding from the head) and iridescent colours. Some, inclu-ding Wilson's Bird-of-paradise, have areas of brightly coloured bare skin – in this case, an extensive area of blue skin on the head.

During his display, the male Wilson's desperately tries to impress the waiting female, dancing back and forth in front of her and displaying all his feathered finery, so that she can evaluate his suitability as a mate. As with all bird courtship, the power rests not with the brightly coloured, dancing male, but with the drab, waiting female: she will make the final decision on which male she will choose to pair up with.

The blue patch of bare skin on the head of the Wilson's Bird-of-paradise adds to its striking looks

Cicinnurus respublica

WILSON'S BIRD-OF-PARADISE

In the Old Testament Book of Genesis, Noah sends forth a Raven, 'which went to and fro, until the waters were dried up from off the earth'. In doing so, the largest member of the crow family achieved the honour of being the very first bird mentioned in the Bible.

Since then, the Raven has featured more times in mythology and folklore than almost any other species, often denoting something sinister, unpleasant – even evil. The most famous incarnation is in the work of Edgar Allan Poe, whose poem 'The Raven', published in 1845, is one of the classics of the Gothic Horror genre. Almost 150 years later, it even inspired a Halloween episode of *The Simpsons*.

In Norse mythology, the God Odin was known as the 'raven god', with two Ravens that perched on his shoulders and told him what was going on in the wider world. Raven mythology is widespread across the species' range, from Ireland and Scandinavia to Asia and North America. In the Pacific northwest, Native Americans believed that Ravens could change their shape or form, and were to be avoided as evil spirits.

In Britain, more place-names commemorate this species than any other: close study of the Ordnance Survey maps that cover the upland regions of the country, especially those of the

The Raven has been featured in mythology and folklore since it appeared in the Bible

Lake District, reveals many examples such as 'Ravenscar', 'Ravenglass' and 'Ravenscraig' – the last denoting a regular nesting site.

Ravens are adaptable birds, found across much of Europe, Asia and North America. Yet, despite being found as far south as Nicaragua and Morocco, they are also one of the few species hardy enough to over-winter in the Arctic.

The key to the Raven's success is an omnivorous diet and opportunistic feeding methods – including scavenging, foraging and when necessary killing its prey. Ravens will hide food in caches when it is plentiful, then retrieve it during times of scarcity. Like other members of its family it has adapted well to living alongside man, exploiting landfill sites for easily obtainable food, though it has also been persecuted by farmers and land owners.

Perhaps the Raven's most remarkable trait, however, is its high intelligence. Ravens are one of the few birds regularly to 'play': in Scotland and Canada they have been seen tobogganing down snow-covered hillsides, apparently purely for fun. One observer noted a whole range of play activities, including swinging while hanging upside down, tugs-of-war, snow-bathing, talon-locking with its siblings in flight, and upside-down gliding in updraughts. None of these had any obvious evolutionary benefit, yet they were still pursued with great enthusiasm.

NORTHERN RAVEN | *Corvus corax*

RAVENS ARE NOT ONLY THE LARGEST OF THEIR FAMILY, THEY ARE ALSO THE LARGEST OF THE WORLD'S 6,000 OR SO SPECIES OF PASSERINE, OR PERCHING BIRDS

Mostly black in plumage, 'true crows' are often associated with sinister or evil in folklore. Yet this group of birds, for so long either ignored or condemned, includes one of the most skilled users of tools in the animal kingdom: the New Caledonian Crow. As its name suggests, this species is found only on the archipelago of New Caledonia, in the northwestern Pacific Ocean.

Like other crows, there is nothing particularly remarkable about this bird's general appearance. Medium-sized by crow standards (about 40 cm long), it is basically black, with glossy feathers. A closer look, however, reveals the distinctive shape of its bill: the lower mandible is set at an upward angle, giving the bill a chisel-like appearance.

This peculiar feature is the key to the crow's ability. When feeding, it will find a small stick or twig, and shape the tip into a hook or barb, which it then uses to extract juicy insect grubs out of holes and cavities in logs of wood.

In doing so, it has the distinction of being the only non-human species with the ability not only to use tools (as, for example, do Chimpanzees and the Woodpecker Finch of the Galápagos) but to *make* them as well. And it does so using a variety of materials and methods: for example, some birds make tools from the thorny edges of the *Pandanus* tree.

Despite their remarkable tool-using skills, New Caledonian Crows also use a wide variety of other feeding methods, including catching insects in flight, raiding other birds' nests for eggs and chicks, and dropping snails onto a hard surface in order to extract them from their shells.

One scientific study set out to determine whether the birds' tool-using behaviour was essentially instinctive – like the ability of a spider to weave a complex web – or whether higher thought processes were at work. The researchers soon discovered that the crows possess the ability to adapt different tools for different situations, confirming that they are displaying something very similar to human intelligence – the ability to solve problems.

Further, because the crows are able to pass on knowledge of how to design and make tools within their social groups, they effectively have a culture of 'tool technology' – just like us! This is all the more remarkable when we consider that the most recent common ancestor of birds and humans lived over 300 million years ago.

The New Caledonian Crow using a tool it has made

Corvus moneduloides | NEW CALEDONIAN CROW

THE WORLD'S 45 OR SO SPECIES OF 'TRUE CROW', IN THE GENUS *CORVUS*, MAKE UP FOR IN INTELLIGENCE WHAT THEY LACK IN BEAUTY

Named after Jared P. Kirtland, the 19th-century naturalist whose son-in-law, Charles Pease, first discovered the bird, Kirtland's Warbler is one of the largest and most striking of the North American warblers. Males have a blue-grey head, streaked back, lemon-yellow underparts and a whitish ring around the eye, and can also be identified by their habit of vigorously pumping their tails up and down.

Of all the 60 or so species of New World warbler found in North America, Kirtland's Warbler now has the unenviable distinction of being the rarest and most endangered. Fewer than 1,500 singing males survive in their specialised Jack Pine habitat in the state of Michigan, and despite having recovered from a low of fewer than 170 singing males during the 1970s and 1980s, the species is still on the critical list.

The problem is that this little bird is very fussy about where it lives, only nesting on the ground in Jack Pine forests between 5 and 20 years of age, and more than 35 hectares in area. The wintering range is also extremely limited: the birds are only found on two island groups in the Caribbean, the Bahamas and the Turks and Caicos Islands.

The reason for the Kirtland's Warbler's original decline was that the Jack Pine forests where it breeds had been left to their own devices, with not enough fires and cutting to help them regenerate. Once the bird's special requirements were understood, a programme of tree-felling and controlled burning helped to create suitable habitat, and the population began to recover.

Despite the conservationists' best efforts, however, Kirtland's Warbler continues to face two major threats, both indirectly created by human beings. The first problem is the arrival in the warbler's range of the Brown-headed Cowbird, a highly opportunistic nest parasite. Originally confined to western North America, the cowbird has spread eastwards in recent decades, largely due to man's clearance of wooded areas for agriculture. Cowbirds are able to lay up to 36 eggs in a single breeding season, posing a major threat to the breeding success of the warblers.

The other problem is even more serious. Global climate change is already having a major effect on the distribution and composition of forests, including the highly specialised habitat of Kirtland's Warbler. Should the Jack Pines become unsuitable for the warbler to breed, it is unlikely to find an alternative, and this attractive little bird will head rapidly towards extinction.

A Kirtland's Warbler on a Jack Pine in its favourite habitat

Dendroica kirtlandii | # KIRTLAND'S WARBLER

KIRTLAND'S WARBLER IS A TEXTBOOK EXAMPLE OF HOW TO USE MODERN CONSERVATION METHODS TO BRING A SPECIES BACK FROM THE BRINK OF EXTINCTION

Darwin's finches, a group of just over a dozen closely related species of finch mainly found on the Galápagos Islands, are probably the best known example of a rapid form of evolution known as 'adaptive radiation'.

They were able to fill vacant ecological niches because of the lack of competition on these remote oceanic islands. This meant that having colonised the archipelago (almost certainly from the South American mainland), the ancestors of these little birds could respond very rapidly to external factors such as habitat, climate and food supply. The result was that one ancestral finch eventually split into the wide range of different species we see today.

The term 'Darwin's finches' was not applied to the group until 1936, about a century after Charles Darwin first observed the birds. Indeed, although it is popularly believed that they inspired Darwin's theory of evolution by natural selection, he actually had no idea that the birds were closely related to each other until after he returned from the *Beagle's* long voyage, when the British ornithologist John Gould pointed it out to him. By this time, however, it was too late to do a proper study of the complex relationships between the different kinds of finch.

One of fourteen of Darwin's Finches — the Common Cactus Finch

Currently, scientists recognise 14 species of Darwin's finches, 13 of which live on the various islands of the Galápagos and one on Cocos Island off the coast of Costa Rica. They fill a wide range of niches: some feed on the ground, while others prefer a more arboreal existence. One of them, the Woodpecker Finch, is able to use small sticks as tools to prise insects out of their holes.

The most interesting feature of these birds is that within each subgroup the different species are distinguished mainly by the size of their bills, which govern what type of prey they are able to feed on. Thus there are Small, Medium and Large Ground-finches, and Small, Medium and Large Tree-finches. The differences between some species are so subtle that even experienced naturalists find identification of individuals with certainty impossible in the field.

Following an episode of the climatic phenomenon El Niño in 1982, exceptionally wet conditions followed by an equally extreme drought led to something even more extraordinary. As a result of these sudden changes in environmental conditions, the Medium Ground-finch evolved a smaller bill to avoid competition for food with invading flocks of Large Ground-finches.

This happened more rapidly than evolutionary changed had been supposed to, and led to a complete rethink about the speed at which natural selection can take place. Thus, almost two centuries after Darwin originally discovered them, the group of finches that bear his name is still making the headlines.

DARWIN'S FINCHES | *genera Geospiza, Camarhynchus, Certhidea and Pinaroloxias*

DESPITE SHARING A COMMON ANCESTOR, THEY HAVE EVOLVED — OVER A RELATIVELY SHORT SPACE OF TIME — TO FILL A VARIETY OF VACANT ECOLOGICAL NICHES

Staring for hours across the baking savannah of East Africa can lead to hallucinations, especially under the searing heat of the midday sun. So imagine the reaction of the first person ever to set eyes on a Long-tailed Paradise-whydah, its tail-feathers hanging down behind its body, as it fluttered over the grassy plains in full display flight. Even today, observers seeing this extraordinary bird for the very first time often find it hard to believe their eyes.

The Long-tailed Paradise-whydah is found across a broad swathe of sub-Saharan Africa, from Senegal in the west to Somalia in the east, with its stronghold on the wide open savannahs of East Africa – hence one of its alternative names, Acacia Paradise-whydah (the other is Eastern Paradise-whydah). It is one of about 20 species in the family Viduidae, commonly known as indigobirds and whydahs, though they are sometimes also referred to as 'widows' or 'widow-finches'.

There are two theories about the origin of the name. Most believe it originates from the long black tail-feathers, similar in appearance to the clothes worn by a widow during a period of mourning; others suggest that it is a corruption of Ouidah, a town in Benin, West Africa, where members of the family were first discovered.

To further confuse the picture, another, closely related group

The distinctive plumes of a male Long-tailed Paradise-whydah in breeding plumage

of birds in the weaver family are officially known as widowbirds, though these too are sometimes called whydahs. One member of this family, the Long-tailed Widowbird, not only has a similar name to this species, but also sports an exceedingly long set of tail-feathers used prominently in display.

The extraordinary jet-black plumes of the male Long-tailed Paradise-whydah are up to 23 cm long, making up almost two-thirds of his total length. He also has a very distinctive plumage: a black face and head contrasting with an orange collar, red breast and pale yellow belly. The female could hardly be more different: small, chunky and sparrow-like, with streaky upperparts and plain, pale underparts. Outside the breeding season the male dispenses with the finery of his tail plumes and closely resembles the female – presumably to reduce the chances of being caught by predators.

Like other members of its family, the Long-tailed Paradise-whydah is one of only about 100 species of bird in the world which practise a strategy known as brood parasitism. This involves laying their eggs in other birds' nests, and allowing the unsuspecting host parents to do all the hard work raising the young. As with many brood parasites (the Common Cuckoo is a well-known exception), the Long-tailed Paradise-whydah only parasitises a single host species, in this case a tiny estrildid finch, the Green-winged Pytilia (or Melba Finch, as it sometimes known).

LONG-TAILED PARADISE-WHYDAH | *Vidua interjecta*

The inclusion of the humble House Sparrow in a book limited to just 100 of the world's most remarkable birds may raise a few eyebrows. But consider the facts. This member of a rather undistinguished group of Old World seedeaters has – thanks to its ability to live alongside human beings – spread to six of the world's seven continents, as a result becoming one of the commonest birds in the world.

One example of the extraordinary adaptability of the House Sparrow sums up its pioneering nature. In the late 1970s, coal miners in Yorkshire were amazed to discover that a small group of sparrows had somehow entered the shaft of their mine, reaching a depth of 600 m beneath the earth's surface. Not only were the sparrows apparently thriving (having been fed by the miners), but one pair even managed to breed and raise three young.

The species has shown a similar tenacity in its ability to spread around the world, either with deliberate or accidental help from humans. In North America, flocks of House Sparrows were released in the middle decades of the 19th century, apparently in order to control invertebrate pests.

They may have managed to do so, but in the absence of competition they soon became a pest themselves – one of only three bird species not officially protected

The male House Sparrow in flight – a bird to be found on six of the seven continents

in the United States (the others being the introduced European Starling and Feral Pigeon). Today, with a population of 400 million or more, the House Sparrow vies with native species such as the Red-winged Blackbird for the title of the commonest North American bird.

The familiar chirping of House Sparrows can also be heard by homesick Europeans in such far-flung locations as Patagonia, Cape Town and Sydney.

Yet at the same time, House Sparrows are showing worrying signs of major population declines in parts of their native range, especially in the Netherlands and Britain. Urban sparrows appear to be suffering most: once so common in central London that birds could be hand-fed in any of the capital's parks, sparrows are now virtually extinct there, just managing to hang on at a few sites such as London Zoo.

A wide range of possible causes has been suggested, from a chemical in unleaded petrol to modern house-building methods, which create fewer places for birds to nest. The reasons are likely to be more complex, involving changes in the countryside as well as in the cities themselves. But whatever the cause, the disappearance of the House Sparrows has had one ironic benefit: few people now take them for granted, as they once used to.

By any definition, therefore, the House Sparrow fully deserves the description 'remarkable'.

HOUSE SPARROW | *Passer domesticus*

HOUSE SPARROWS HAVE USED THEIR ABILITY TO FIND FOOD AND NESTING PLACES
AROUND OUR HOMES AS A PASSPORT TO GLOBAL SUCCESS

No book on the world's birds can hope to include a definitive – or even a reasonably complete – reading list, as there are so many subjects, regions and countries. Instead I have compiled a representative selection of books. Some will be obtainable in high-street bookshops, or by mail order from Subbuteo Books (www.wildlifebooks.com) or the Natural History Book Service (www.nhbs.com). Several are major, multi-volume handbooks – you may wish to access them as reference books from libraries.

Handbook of the Birds of the World, **Josep del Hoyo, Andrew Elliott et al., 1992–present (Lynx Edicions)**
With 16 volumes, of which 11 have appeared so far, this is by far the most comprehensive work on the world's birds. Fabulous photographs, excellent illustrations, authoritative text. Truly remarkable!

Collins Birds of the World, **Les Beletsky, 2007 (HarperCollins)**
Single volume covering all the world's 200 or so bird families. Excellent value.

Birds Britannica, **Mark Cocker & Richard Mabey, 2005 (Chatto & Windus)**
Wonderful compendium of folklore and modern anecdotes about Britain's birdlife.

Collins Bird Guide, **Lars Svensson, Peter J. Grant, Killian Mullarney and Dan Zetterstrom, 2001 (HarperCollins)**
The definitive field guide to the birds of Europe, North Africa and the Middle East.

The Birds of the Western Palearctic, **David Snow, Christopher M. Perrins, 1999 (OUP)**
Multi-volume work on the birds of Europe, North Africa and the Middle East. Also available on CD-Rom and in a concise version.

Birds of Africa, **C. Hilary Fry, Stuart Keith et al., 1997–2004 (Academic Press/Poyser/Christopher Helm Publishers)**
A magnificent seven-volume work.

Handbook of Australian, New Zealand and Antarctic Birds, **Royal Australasian Ornithologists Union, 1990–2006 (OUP Australia/New Zealand)**
Multi-volume work on the birds of two contrasting continents.

Threatened Birds of the World, **A. Stattersfield, D. Capper, 2000 (BirdLife International)**
Details of over one thousand species of bird currently under threat.

FURTHER READING

BirdLife International

BirdLife is a global alliance of conservation organisations that share the same mission: to conserve wild birds, their habitats and global biodiversity. As a worldwide community, we work together across a wide range of conservation actions – from working with governments on global issues like climate change, to local actions like protecting individual species and their habitats.

With around 2.5 million members and 8 million supporters worldwide, our network of more than 100 national organisations forms the world's leading authority on the status of birds, their habitats and the issues and threats facing bird life.

The future of the world's 10,000 species of birds is inextricably linked to the welfare and livelihoods of people. One in eight bird species is threatened with extinction; the loss of even one diminishes us all. The BirdLife network is working to build a better future for birds and people.

How you can help BirdLife:

There are many ways in which you can help fund our work and every donation however large or small makes a difference.

BirdLife urgently need your donations towards our Species Champions initiative if we are to save the 189 Critically Endangered species most at risk of global extinction. Many of these birds could become extinct within the next ten years.

BirdLife and its Partners know what needs to be done. What we need are the funds to make it happen.

- $20 can pay for 100 seedlings for a reforestation project in Africa to improve the natural habitat for rare birds
- $300 can buy 1 hectare of forest to protect at least one pair of globally threatened birds in Asia
- $1,000 can pay for vital field equipment to help conservationists in the Middle East
- $2,000+ can pay for a habitat survey in South America

If you are a resident of the US, please make cheques payable to American Friends of BirdLife International Inc and post to American Friends Of BirdLife Inc, c/o Chapel & York, PMB #293, 601 Pennsylvania Ave. NW, Ste 900, South Bldg., Washington DC 20004. American Friends is an independent charitable organisation with separate 501 (c) 3 status which enables US residents to receive direct tax benefits for contributions to the work of BirdLife International.

UK residents – please make your cheques payable to BirdLife International and post to BirdLife International, Wellbrook Court, Girton Road, Cambridge, CB3 0NA.

Alternatively you can donate securely on line by visiting www.birdlife.org and click on 'How to help'.

For more information please e-mail howtohelp@birdlife.org or telephone +44 (0)1223 277318.

BIRDLIFE INTERNATIONAL

INDEX

Note: page numbers in bold refer to photographs

PICTURE CREDITS